Neeley Never Said Goodbye

Carole Gift Page

MOODY PRESS

CHICAGO

*To Doris Elaine Fell and Sheila
Cragg, who share so generously of
their wisdom and editorial skills and
who relentlessly demand of me my best*

© 1984, 1991 by
CAROLE GIFT PAGE

Revised edition

ISBN: 0-8024-8454-9

1 2 3 4 5 6 Printing/LC/Year 94 93 92 91

Printed in the United States of America

1

I am in the mall, walking on a foot-wide cinderblock wall, my arms outstretched, balancing as if I were walking a tightrope. I feel cool and funny and daring—and a little embarrassed. I am wearing my wild, glittery, oversized sweatshirt hand-painted by yours truly with squiggles and curlicues and pennants and stars, and Richard's name scrawled across the front in giant, red-hot letters.

Richard thinks I'm crazy. He calls me the dizzy, daft, moonstruck Holly Rhoades. Richard would never wear anyone's name on his clothes. Richard is almost sixteen and would never wear garish graffiti on his T-shirt or neon laces in his L.A. Gears.

But actually, Richard is crazier than I am. We hang out together. He's the funniest guy I know. Totally quirky. Maybe that's why I like him so much—not mushy boyfriend stuff exactly—I'm only fourteen going on fifteen, after all, and my folks have said positively no serious dating until I'm sixteen. But it's like Richard and I know without saying it that someday we'll be more than friends.

But I can't think about that right now. I must concentrate on this high wall, on not falling off, on walking with a little class so I don't come across looking like a geek with two left feet.

You see, Richard is videotaping me. He's got his Camcorder perched on his shoulder like a natural appendage. (My dad's description of Richard: "Doesn't that camera-crazed boy go anywhere without that thing on his shoulder?'' My dad hates being videotaped.)

I don't mind starring in Richard's homemade videos, as long as I look cool, as long as Richard doesn't catch me first thing in the morning when I look like Dracula's mother in hot rollers. Actually, Richard tells me I look like Molly Ringwald's younger sister—if she has a younger sister. Or maybe he's just being kind.

Whoops! Suddenly, I lose my balance. My arms flail the air as I totter momentarily, my heart racing. But my trusty Reeboks grip the cement, and I catch my footing. Richard, oblivious of my near calamity, looks up from his Camcorder and shouts, ''Hey, Holly, do something dramatic. Hop on one leg. Try a cartwheel!''

''On this narrow wall? Get real!''

''I need more action, Holly. This'll never cut it. Do your Lucy imitation. Pretend you're on a high-rise ledge washing windows. Or in a big vat in Greece trampling grapes.''

For half a second I imagine myself doing Lucy on this wall. Nev-er! ''You're a real nut case, Richard! A real nut case!''

''Come on, Holly, I need something sensational, earth-shattering, trend-setting—''

I put my hands on my hips and give Richard my most devastating glare. ''I know you, Richard. I know what you're after. You want funny footage for that home video show on TV. You want destruction, catastrophe, humiliation. Totally bizarre behavior. Why, I'd have to slip on a banana peel, or fall on my head, or break my neck to get on that show!''

''Would you mind, Holly?''

I stick out my tongue and give him my loudest raspberry sound. ''That's what I think of your home videos, Richard Hogan!''

''I was kidding, Holly. Just kidding!'' He puts the camera down and grins. Richard has the warmest, crinkliest eyes I've ever seen and a thatch of caramel-brown hair that forever falls over his shaggy eyebrows. Sometimes he reminds me of one of those cute mop dogs with eyes you can't see under all that hair, but I'd never tell him that. I can never stay mad at Richard.

6

I climb down off the wall and brush off my jeans. "Know what we need? A double frozen yogurt with caramel topping, hot fudge, and slivered almonds."

"Eat that, and you'll need a stomach pump."

"Come on. It's healthy."

"Wheat germ and sunflower seeds are healthy."

"If you're a tree."

"Right. Let's go for the frozen yogurt."

We amble through the mall to the yogurt shop and spend the next half hour consuming our luscious frozen desserts. Actually, Richard devours his, I *savor* mine. I like to let the icy smoothness roll over my tongue and slide down my throat. Richard sits and watches and drums his fingers on the table. He hates waiting. He accuses me of eating like Princess Di—all fancy and deliberate, with my little pinky crooked just so. But Richard positively inhales his food. One minute it's there, the next minute it's gone.

"What time do you have to be home?" he asks, looking at his watch.

"I don't know. Soon. Before dark."

"Your folks won't be home yet, will they?"

"No. They're both working, as usual."

"So there's no rush."

"My brother, Neeley, will be home."

"So? He's a big boy, three years older than you. A senior, even. He can take care of himself."

"I know. I just like to be there. In case he needs me."

Richard makes a face. I can't tell whether he's amused or irritated. "I never knew a girl like you, Holly."

I wrinkle my nose. "Really? Why?"

He shrugs. "Most girls hate their brothers."

"Not me. I love Neeley. He's special."

"Yeah, I know. He's an artist. But he's also moody. And a loner."

"That's called artistic temperament."

"Really? I thought it was called ill humor."

I swallow the last spoonful of my yogurt. "You know, Richard, sometimes I think you don't like Neeley."

7

He frowns. Richard hardly ever frowns. He mutters, "Sometimes I think there's such a thing as being *too* devoted."

I laugh. "Richard, you actually sound jealous. He's my big *brother*, for goodness sake! Of course, I'm, uh, what you said."

"Devoted."

"You make it sound like a dirty word."

"Maybe 'obsessed' is a better word."

I crumple my paper napkin and throw it at Richard. "I am not obsessed. I am definitely not obsessed. Crazy people are obsessed."

"OK, that was a poor word choice. I'm sorry."

"You should be. Maybe you're just jealous that Neeley and I have such a good relationship."

"Get real, Holly. He still teases you. I've heard him."

"I know. I do get mad at him, and sometimes I'd like to wring his neck." I draw in a long, slow breath. "But I—I'd die if anything ever happened to him."

"Well, such loyalty is rare," Richard says dryly. "My sister, Gail, totally hates me."

"She does not! Your sister's nice. She always smiles and talks to me when I come over."

"Sure. You're a girl. Gail doesn't want you to know she's a dweeb. But when she and I are alone, it's the pits."

"What does she do?"

"Well, for starters, when she cooks, she gives me the burned hamburger. And the stale bun. She tapes her dumb soap operas over my videotapes. And she lends my Amy Grant tapes to her friends. And, worst, she leaves my side of the bathroom a disgusting mess."

I laugh. "Sounds like sour grapes to me. What do you do to her?"

"Nothing much. Just little things. Like videotaping her and her friends coloring their hair. It turned out a putrid purple once! And at their slumber party I taped them at dawn in their sleeping bags. Uh, you know Kristy Collins?"

"The prom queen? Of course. She's gorgeous."

"Not at six in the morning without her face and fancy hair-do."

"Richard, you're terrible!"

"I know. That's what I love about me."

I give him a grudging smile. "Know what I love about you?"

His eyes crinkle. "My flawless good looks?"

"No. You're funny. You always make me laugh."

"OK, so I'm good for a laugh. Life could be worse."

We leave the yogurt shop and head home, walking leisurely. On the way, Richard spots something—a cat in a tree. His eagle eye is always on the lookout for something to film. He whips his Camcorder into place like a cowboy pulling his gun from his holster and takes aim.

"Wait, Richard," I insist. "The poor little thing is stuck. He can't get down."

"I know. It's a real heart-tugger. I'm zooming in for a closeup."

"Well, we can't just leave him there. He's hardly more than a kitten. Listen, Richard, he's mewing!"

"Quiet, Holly. I wanna catch the sound on my microphone."

I step in front of Richard's camera and grab the lowest tree limb. I hoist myself up, digging my Reeboks into the rough bark. I reach for the next limb, and the next. I haven't climbed a tree since I was ten, but it must be one of those things you never forget, because suddenly there I am up beside that trembling little fluffball of a kitten. With my left arm circling the tree trunk, I reach cautiously for the frightened little creature. He hisses and bats at my hand with a tiny gray paw. I gather him up anyway and hold him against my chest. He's all warm fur and shivers and whiskers. He starts to purr, and two big velvet-green eyes look up trustingly at me. "I've got him, Richard!" I call triumphantly.

"Terrific! Now come down slowly, and keep your face to the camera. Who knows? This rescue might make it on TV's 'Nine One One' show! You'll be a hero, Holly."

"That's me," I giggle. "Holly Rhoades, the Great Rescuer. Champion of the underdog—er, under*cat*."

9

2

Mario the plumber is passing through Darkland on his way to rescue the Princess . . .

I watch my older brother, Neeley, sitting on the edge of the couch, leaning intently toward the video screen. He works the controller with an intensity that makes me uncomfortable—as if his life depends on it.

"Oops, you lost," I tell him. "You'll never rescue the Princess."

Neeley swears and tosses the controller aside.

"Don't let Mom hear you say that," I warn. "She'll wash your mouth out with soap."

"Oh, Holly, she stopped doing that years ago." With an impatient hand he pushes back his dark brown hair from his forehead.

"Well, Mom'll do something. She won't let you go out with Marsha," I argue, knowing the threat is outrageous. Mom knows true love when she sees it and isn't about to interfere in Neeley's romance of the century.

"Take a hike, squirt," says Neeley. He stands up to his full six feet and smooths the knees of his worn Levi's.

"I already did. To the mall. With Richard."

"That why you're late? You were with that nerd Richard Hogan?"

"Nope. I was up a tree with a cat."

"Be serious!"

"Why? You're serious enough for both of us."

"Gimme a break, Holly."

"Wanna play another game of Super Mario Brothers?" I ask, changing the subject.

"Nope. Got a date."

"On a school night?"

"We're going to the library to study."

"Fer sure. And I'm the Queen of England."

"Lay off," he snaps, "or you'll be a kid sister with her braces wrapped around her ears."

I follow Neeley into the kitchen. He picks up a ripe banana from the fruit bowl and begins peeling it. "Why do you have to see Marsha tonight?" I persist. "You saw her last night."

Neeley teasingly stuffs half the banana into my mouth. "What you got against Marsha, half-pint?"

I chew, swallow hard, and reply, "Marsha thinks she's God's gift to men."

"She is . . . to *me*."

"I hate the way she lolls in front of a mirror, smiling at herself like a Cheshire cat." I'm talking over the banana-lump in my throat. I don't sound the least bit convincing, even to myself.

"You're just jealous," argues Neeley, "because she's got curves where you've got—"

"Neeley Rhoades, if you say Dad's handkerchiefs, I'll wring your neck!"

"So that's your secret!" he laughs. I start laughing too. I can never stay angry at Neeley for very long.

He squeezes the back of my neck and bends his face close to mine. "I'll tell you my secret if you promise not to blab," he says conspiratorially.

I look up eagerly. "I never told Mom you put Kool-Aid in her vitamin capsules when you were ten."

"Only because I didn't tell Dad you stuffed Play-Doh down the barrel of his favorite hunting rifle."

"Well, it was *your* Play-Doh."

Neeley shrugs. "I was creating a great work of art, Holly, while you were a runny-nosed little kid bent on mischief and destruction."

I jut out my lower lip. "Mom says we're just alike. I'm running three years behind you is all."

"Not much alike. You're no artist," claims Neeley, only half in jest. He softens the remark with, "Of course, you've got other talents—"

"I know. All hidden."

"You bake a great pizza," he offers. His idea of a truce.

I take an apple from the fruit bowl and shine it on my shirttail—actually Neeley's shirttail. I love the roomy comfort of Neeley's old, outgrown shirts. I bite slowly into the apple, not eager to let him off the hook.

"Sometimes it's better to have no talent at all," he continues, "than not enough to be the best."

"You are the best," I say, forgetting my wounded pride. "Everyone at Jefferson High says you're the best artist they ever had."

"What would a mere ninth grader know?" he teases.

"I know you're going to be a famous artist someday."

Neeley scowls. "No, Holly. I'm good but not the best."

I peer intently at him and ask, "How come you're so touchy lately, Neeley?"

"As if you didn't know. I already got two rejections from the art schools I applied to."

"Yeah, I know, but you've still got two more to hear from."

"Fat chance I have, the way things are going."

I decide not to press the subject. Neeley has a way of clamming up sometimes so that no one can reach him. I don't want to see that door shut in his eyes now, blocking me out. So I say lightly, "What's this big dark secret you have to tell me?"

The solemn creases in Neeley's face spring back into beautiful laugh lines. His dark eyes glint with merriment. "Oh yes, my secret," he says slyly. With a flourish he removes his high school class ring and flips it in the air. "Guess who's getting this tonight!"

"Not Marsha."

"Yes—Marsha."

"Does she know?"

"Not yet."

"But you *love* that ring. And this is your senior year. You should wear it yourself."

Neeley looks away and in a voice I can scarcely hear, murmurs, "I love Marsha more."

I look closely at Neeley. Did I hear right? I have never before heard him say he loved anyone. "You love . . . Marsha?" I repeat dubiously.

He gives me a warning glance. "You tell anyone, and I tell the world you're crazy in love with good ol' video whiz Richard."

"I am not! But you—you really love Marsha?"

He brushes off my question with a flippant, "So long, kiddo. Keep good thoughts for me, OK?" With that he slings his rumpled leather jacket over his shoulder and heads for the door in his lanky stride.

In grudging silence I watch him go. *I'll keep lousy thoughts for that catty, conniving Marsha Piper*, I resolve. Neeley is my only brother, the best brother in the world, even if sometimes he is a tease. I'm not about to relinquish his affection to an airhead like Marsha Piper!

3

Neeley is home early from his date with Marsha. He shuffles in the door, his shoulders drooping, his hands buried deep in his jacket pockets.

I am stretched out on the couch doing my algebra homework and watching a "Family Ties" rerun. Neeley walks right by me as if I don't exist. I reach out and catch his arm teasingly. "How'd it go with Marsha?"

He whirls around as if he's been struck and growls, "Knock it off, will ya?"

"Excuse me for living," I say, sitting up. A dark frown remains etched on Neeley's features. "What'd you two have for dinner?" I ask. "Sour lemons?"

Neeley ignores my sarcasm. "Where's Mom and Dad?" he says, removing his jacket and tossing it on a chair.

"Dad's out selling insurance as usual, and Mom's showing a house."

"This late?"

"She called from the real estate office and said she's hoping to close a deal tonight. She doesn't know how long it will take."

Neeley drops down in Dad's easy chair and sprawls his long legs out, propping them on the coffee table. I see his jaw moving slightly and know he is grinding his teeth. When we were little kids and shared the same bedroom, I could hear Neeley gritting his teeth in his sleep. Our dentist said he had worn down three teeth that way. I glance at Neeley's right hand. He is still wearing his class ring. I summon my most sympathetic tone and ask, "What happened with Marsha?"

Neeley grumbles, "What makes you think something happened?"

"You've still got your ring."

He twists it unconsciously on his finger. "She didn't want my ring," he says, looking past me.

I feel Neeley's pain like a splinter under my nail. "Didn't want it?" I echo. "How could she not want it?"

"She doesn't want to go steady," he says, his voice a rueful monotone. "She says going steady is old-fashioned."

"But you've been dating for six months," I argue. "I thought you were in love."

Neeley jumps up and mutters rawly, "Yeah, me too." He grabs his jacket, throws it over his shoulder, and takes big steps across the room.

"Where are you going?" I ask, standing up.

"To my room. I've got sketches to do for art tomorrow."

Lamely I call after him. "Marsha's not good enough for you anyway. She's stuck up and flirty and fickle!" Neeley doesn't hear me. He has already taken the stairs two at a time up to his room. I hear his door slam hard behind him.

I sit back down on the couch and pick up my algebra book. I don't feel like studying now. I feel sad and empty inside. I wish Neeley would have stayed and talked. I wish I could have said something to help him. Fleetingly I consider going up to his room and knocking on his door. But once Neeley's door is closed he might as well be behind the Great Wall of China. So I sink back against the cushions, prop my algebra book open, and promptly lapse into a daydream.

I remember Neeley when he was happy and carefree and not as intense as he is these days. I recall the times we hiked in the woods and he drew charcoal sketches for me of frisky squirrels, spring flowers, and weeping willow trees. Last summer he taught my friend Lori and me how to swim. On hot summer days we bicycled to the beach and swam for hours until we were sunburned and exhausted. In those days I felt like Neeley's best friend. He didn't mind my being a tagalong. He laughingly called himself a loner and said he didn't like running with a bunch of guys or playing baseball or soccer. He would rather sit by himself and sketch or paint. My girlfriends were actually jealous that I had such a great brother—one who treated me like a real *person*.

Neeley still treats me OK, but things aren't like they used to be. Not since Marsha. She has changed Neeley. It isn't just his art that obsesses him now. It's Marsha. Marsha this and Marsha that. He lives for her. Who would believe she would be such a dork and cast him aside like yesterday's garbage? I hate her!

My daydream has turned dark. Anger is churning inside me. I imagine myself yanking Marsha's permed black hair and slapping her perfectly made-up face. But my visions of sweet revenge are punctured by the sound of the front door opening and closing. Dad comes in looking tired and preoccupied. He removes his overcoat and hangs it in the hall closet, then looks my way. "Hi, hon. Your mother home?"

"No. She's showing a house."

"Great scott. I suppose that means no dinner."

"Mom said you wouldn't be home in time anyway."

"I was counting on heating up the leftovers."

"I had a TV dinner."

"What about Neeley?"

"He was out with Marsha tonight."

"Is he still out?"

"No, he's up in his room." I consider telling Dad about Marsha rejecting Neeley's class ring, but Dad doesn't look in the mood to discuss Neeley's love life tonight. Instead, I ask conversationally, "Did you sell lots of insurance?"

Dad's voice is tight. "I didn't meet my quota, if that's what you mean." He sits down in his chair and picks up the newspaper. His eyes look shadowed, the creases deeper than usual.

"Do you want me to put a TV dinner in the microwave for you?" I ask.

"No, hon. Thanks, but I'll fix a sandwich later." He opens the paper and raises it so I can't see his face anymore. I turn back to my algebra book. I still have nine problems to solve. But I'm in no mood for homework. I'll call Richard instead. He'll say something funny and make me laugh. Right now I can't think of anything I need more.

16

4

Morning. I awake to the delicious aromas of sizzling bacon, coffee, and blueberry muffins. I pull on my pink robe and scurry downstairs. Mom is at the stove, already dressed for work, her shoulder-length brown hair combed back neatly and clipped behind her neck. She looks up and smiles. "Hungry?"

"Starved!" I carry the butter and muffins over to the table. "What's the special occasion?" I ask.

"No occasion," says Mom. Lowering her voice, she admits, "I felt a little guilty about leaving you all on your own for dinner last night. Your father wasn't too happy about it."

I shrug. "You had to work. Dad's late all the time."

"But he's not the chief cook and bottle washer," says Mom wryly.

Dad enters the kitchen then and gives Mom a peck on the cheek. "What's this about bottle washers?" he quizzes, pulling back his chair.

Mom and I exchange amused glances. "Just an inside joke, Dad."

He glances around. "Neeley up yet?"

"Nope."

"Well, it would be nice if we'd all have a meal together for a change," he says. He goes to the foot of the stairs and calls Neeley's name. Minutes later Neeley meanders into the kitchen. His dark hair is mussed, he's still in his pajamas, and his expression is as gloomy as it was last night.

"Are you feeling well, Neeley?" asks Mom.

He sits down and spears some bacon onto his plate. "Yeah, sure, I'm fine. Why?"

"You look a little worse for wear, son," Dad observes. "You going to make it to school on time?"

"Yeah, no sweat." He helps himself to the butter.

"We haven't prayed yet," says Mom. "Neeley, would you, please?"

An expression of panic crosses Neeley's face. He replies, "Not this morning, Mom."

"Your mother made a simple request, Neeley." Dad sounds stern.

Neeley looks imploringly at him. "I don't feel like praying this morning, Dad. Is that a crime?"

Dad's nostrils flare slightly. "Since when is thanking God for the food a major problem with you, Neeley?"

Neeley's voice rises precariously. "It's not a problem. Why do you have to make such a big deal out of it?"

Mom interrupts with a sharp, "Stewart, *I'll* pray." We all bow our heads. I don't hear a word Mom says. I figure God would just as soon we had skipped thanking Him this morning.

For a few minutes we all eat in silence. Then Dad looks at Mom and says, "So did you sell a house last night, Marge?"

Mom pokes at the food on her plate. "No, Stewart. I worked on that deal for weeks, and at the last minute it fell through."

"How come?" I ask.

"The people couldn't come up with enough collateral for a loan. These days you have to be wealthy to buy your own home."

"Or to buy a loaf of bread," quips Dad. He glances at Neeley, expecting a smile, but Neeley is scowling over his food. I laugh half-heartedly. Everyone is silent again.

Dad takes a second helping of bacon and eggs, then hands the platter to Neeley. "How was your date with Marsha, son?"

"OK," grunts Neeley.

"It's really not a good idea to date on a school night," continues Dad. "Try not to make it a practice."

I wait for Neeley to tell Mom and Dad about his crisis with Marsha, but he just mutters another, "OK, Dad."

"They were studying," I insert, recalling the reason Neeley had given me.

Dad chuckles. "Yeah, well, I remember what it was like when your Mom and I were dating and studying together. We spent more time studying each other than any textbooks. Right, Marge?"

Mom gives Dad one of her *Oh, Stewart, please!* looks and says, "Well, I was always determined to study no matter what else you had in mind."

Dad changes the subject abruptly with, "How are your studies going, son?"

"All right," Neeley answers without enthusiasm.

"Well, this is your final semester of high school, your last chance to make those grades for college." He sips his coffee, then clears his throat. "The other day I talked with a colleague whose son is going to State next year. The boy's majoring in computer science." When Neeley doesn't respond, Dad continues, slipping unconsciously into his official salesman's voice. "You know, Neeley, computers are the big thing these days. That's where your big money is. It wouldn't hurt you to consider a career in something like computer science."

"I've already picked a career," mumbles Neeley sullenly.

"You mean art? Sure, I know art is important to you. But it's not the sort of thing you can build a life on."

"I'm going to," says Neeley.

"Well, there's teaching, of course," concedes Dad. "Art teachers don't make all that much, but I suppose you could get by."

"Not an art teacher," protests Neeley. "I want to be an artist."

"He wants to be another Michelangelo," I interject.

Neeley gives me a withering glance. I didn't intend my remark to sound so flippant. I know Neeley's artistic idol is Michelangelo. He's never come right out and said he wants to paint another Sistine ceiling or carve the biblical David in marble. But I sense that Neeley's dreams are just as lofty.

19

Dad is speaking again. "What have you heard from the art schools you've applied to?" We all know exactly what Neeley has heard. Dad is obviously rehashing the matter to prove his point.

"I've been rejected by two of them," Neeley says in a sad, thin voice. He looks as if he is shrinking down in his chair. I know he hates Dad's interrogations.

"He still has two more chances," I pipe in. "Besides, he hasn't even heard yet from his favorite choice, the Chicago Art Institute. I bet you anything they accept him."

Dad isn't about to be sidetracked. "Listen to me, Neeley," he says intently. "If it doesn't work out with the art schools, will you apply to State? Get a degree in business administration or computer science, something that will give you a little security." Dad's jaw sags slightly. "Don't get stuck like I did, son. When I was your age I had to go to work to help out at home. My dad was a dreamer and a drifter. I couldn't afford college. Now my choices are limited. I've got a family to support and never enough money to meet all the bills." He looks at Mom. "I never wanted your mother to have to work."

"I don't mind," says Mom. "It just gets on my nerves, trying to balance everything." She gazes wistfully at Neeley and me. "And it doesn't leave me much time or energy to enjoy my kids."

"Will you promise to try State, Neeley?" persists Dad.

Neeley squirms uncomfortably. He twists his mouth as if he is in pain. Finally he says, so low I can barely hear him, "Yeah, OK."

"What? You'll try State?"

"Yeah, but only if the Art Institute doesn't come through."

5

Saturday morning, the first of April. I wake up smiling like the sun beaming through my bedroom window. Easter vacation is here at last!

There is a light tap on my door. Neeley enters with a grin as big as mine. "You look happy," I remark, reaching for my robe.

"I am," he nods, a mysterious glint in his eyes.

"OK, so tell me. You are as glad about spring break as I am?"

Neeley leans against the wall, pretending to be nonchalant. "Yeah, that too."

"But . . . something more?" I coax.

The words spill out. "I've decided to have a positive attitude, you know, about Marsha," he says. "I figure if I give her a little time she'll come around." He steps forward and spreads his arms mockingly. "After all, I'm an irresistible guy, right?"

I pretend to gag. Neeley darts over and shoves my little plastic trash basket under my chin. I push it away. "Stop it, sponge face. I'm not going to throw up."

"You had me fooled." He laughs. He sits down beside me on the bed and studies my face. His expression darkens. "Holly, what in the world happened to you?"

I draw back warily. "What are you talking about?"

"Your eye," he replies with concern. "You sure got a shiner. What'd you do—slug yourself in your sleep? Or did you and Richard have a fight?"

"There's nothing wrong with my eye," I exclaim, touching my cheek cautiously.

Neeley peers more intently. "Why, those red and purple hues are downright inspiring."

I jump off the bed and dash to the mirror. "I can't possibly have a black eye," I cry. "How could I face anyone? What would I—" I stare at my reflection. "Why, there's nothing wrong with my eye, Neeley. You made it up!"

"April Fool!" he howls.

I lunge for my pillow and smack him over the head. He catches the pillow and tosses it back, hitting me square in the face. I recoil momentarily, then regain my balance and swing the pillow vigorously in the air.

Neeley cautions, "If the feathers fly, Mom will have our heads."

"Then off with our heads!" I command in my most menacing Queen of Hearts voice. I let the pillow fly, but Neeley ducks. It hits the door with a thud and bursts open.

"Told you," taunts Neeley.

"Beat it, Neeley Rhoades, or I'll tar and *feather* you!"

"Tar me with what?" he challenges. "Your makeup base?"

"Vanishing cream—if I had any!"

Neeley raises his hands placatingly. "Truce!"

"What for?"

"I came on a friendly mission."

"Sure you did."

"Really. I'm driving into town for some art supplies. Wanna go?"

"Can I drive?"

"Are you kidding?"

"You let me once, remember!"

Neeley scowls. "OK, so I took pity on you and tried to give you a driving lesson. I'm lucky you didn't run us off a cliff."

I settle into a pout. "I thought I did pretty good. Why, I bet I could drive blindfolded."

22

"That's just how it looked, kiddo." Neeley sighs. "So are you going to town with me or not?"

"Can't. Lori's coming over."

"Bring her too."

"OK." I sound casual but I'm already thinking how thrilled Lori will be. Lori Collins is my best friend, and she's been desperately in love with Neeley since third grade. He considers her a second sister, but that doesn't dampen Lori's hopes. She'd give her A average to have a date with Neeley.

Lori arrives at ten sharp. When she learns we're going shopping with Neeley, she rushes to my room and borrows my blush and frosted plum eye shadow. Then she slips her glasses into her purse.

"You won't be able to see anything," I warn.

"Who needs to see?" She pushes back her straight, straw-blonde hair and sucks in her tummy. Lori is a few pounds overweight and on a perpetual diet. One week she eats nothing but tomatoes, another week it's wilted lettuce or cucumber salad.

"What are you eating this week?" I ask.

"Hard-boiled eggs."

"Yuck!"

"I know. I'm seeing yokes in my sleep. But I've lost two pounds."

"I can tell," I say. I can't really, but I know my remark will make Lori's day.

While Lori primps, she leans toward me and whispers confidentially, "I hear Neeley and Marsha broke up."

"Sort of."

"Well, did they or didn't they?"

"She refused his class ring," I reply, "but Neeley thinks she'll change her mind."

Lori pushes at the bridge of her nose where her glasses would have been and nearly pokes herself in the eye.

"They're in your purse," I remind her.

"Yeah, I forgot. Habit, you know."

"So how did you hear about Neeley and Marsha?" I ask.

Lori hesitates. "Last night I saw Marsha at Pietro's Pizza Parlor with David Higgins. They looked pretty friendly."

I clasp Lori's arm. "Please don't tell Neeley. He'd die if he found out she was seeing someone else."

"I won't tell, Holly. You know I couldn't stand to see Neeley hurt."

Our conversation is interrupted by Neeley's impatient voice from downstairs. "Come on, girls! You can gossip in the car!"

We scurry downstairs, purses in hand, sweaters flying over our shoulders. Neeley is standing by the door, tapping his foot. "You two kept me waiting so long you can buy me lunch."

"You can share Lori's," I tease as we walk to the car. "Half a hard-boiled egg."

The joke escapes Neeley. Lori jabs my ribs with her elbow. To make amends, I let Lori sit in the middle between Neeley and me.

Neeley's restored '56 Chevy chugs and sputters as he backs out of the driveway. This car is his prize possession. It's metallic blue and has black imitation fur seat covers, a leather steering wheel, and a red scarf of Marsha's hanging from the mirror.

"So you girls have this Saturday to spend as you please," Neeley remarks, making conversation.

"Well, you know me. My Saturdays are always free," replies Lori. "Dad spends the day working on his sermon, so Mom and I find other things to do."

I nod knowingly. Lori's dad is Pastor Collins, our minister. Lori and I sit together in church, so I'm careful not to fall asleep or whisper or write notes in the bulletin.

When Neeley makes a sharp right turn onto Main Street, Lori allows herself to slide closer to him. She asks him about his latest art project—Neeley's favorite topic next to Marsha.

"I'm doing a sculpture for my senior project," he tells her.

"Oh really?" Lori sounds impressed. "You mean something abstract like—like Henry Moore's *Reclining Figure*."

"Henry Moore?" I echo. "Isn't he that senior with the frizzy orange hair?"

"Henry Moore is a famous English sculptor," Lori explains patiently. Honestly, she knows something about everything!

"He can't be that famous," I grumble. "I never heard of him."

24

"He's done some fantastic work," reflects Neeley, "but I prefer—"

"He adores Michelangelo," I interject. "You know, the guy who painted that fancy ceiling and sculpted all the overweight ladies."

"She means the Sistine Chapel," Neeley explains.

"I know," replies Lori. "I read *The Agony and the Ecstasy* for a book report last year." She pauses, then asks, "Are you going to carve something out of marble?"

"I'd love to carve something out of Carrara marble like Michelangelo used."

"But you'd have to go to Italy for that, wouldn't you?"

"Yeah, well, I'm not much into the subtractive process anyway."

"What do you mean?" Lori is hanging on Neeley's every word.

He pulls into the parking lot and maneuvers into a narrow space. Even after he turns off the engine he is still explaining to Lori the difference between the additive and subtractive processes of sculpture. I'm bored to tears!

"I'll be using a special modeling clay that has great plastic qualities," he continues, his voice earnest and full of purpose.

"What are you going to sculpt?" asks Lori raptly. She knows just the right questions to keep Neeley talking forever.

"A bust," he explains.

I look over, surprised. "I thought you were making a head."

Neeley laughs. "That's what a bust is, dummy. A head and shoulders."

"Then why didn't you say so?" I sink down in the seat and peer at my watch. "It's late, you guys. In case you haven't noticed, the car has stopped."

"Who's posing for you, Neeley?" persists Lori. I could wring her neck for using delaying tactics. Then I wince as a thought occurs to me: I couldn't possibly be jealous of my best friend, could I?

"I was hoping Marsha would pose for me," Neeley explains, "but I don't imagine she could sit still that long."

"And Mom and Dad wouldn't sit still for Marsha camping in your room," I add dryly.

Lori brushes her hair back from her face in a leisurely gesture. "Then you're looking for someone to pose for you, Neeley?"

"No, I'm going to do a self-portrait," he replies. "It'll be a real challenge to capture myself in clay."

"I don't know," I mutter. "I captured you in mud when I was only six."

"Oh, it'll be a wonderful work of art," praises Lori. "But how will you do it?"

"With three mirrors." Neeley's enthusiasm expands by the minute. "I'll put them at just the right angle—like this—" He begins to demonstrate with his hands.

"You guys talk shop," I announce, opening the door and sliding out. "I'm going inside."

Neeley promptly opens his door, helps Lori out, and walks around to my side. "Draw in your claws, half-pint." He squeezes the nape of my neck as if I were an obstreperous kitten.

I retaliate teasingly with, "Keep your grubby hand to yourself, Van Gogh."

As we saunter toward the art supplies store, Neeley swings a comradely arm around Lori's shoulder and mine. "When we're finished here, how about Big Boy's for a double cheeseburger and chocolate malt?"

Lori cuts me off before I can explain about her hard-boiled egg diet. 'I'd love a double cheeseburger," she gushes as she gazes in nearsighted bliss at my gorgeous hunk of a brother.

6

Saterday is here again, drizzly with rain. Tomorrow is Easter. Spring, where are you?

Neeley has spent his entire week of vacation in his room working on his sculpture. He won't let anyone in. I tease him about being a mad scientist concocting a secret brew that will blow up the world. Neeley replies by doing his weird Frankenstein imitation.

But most of the time Neeley doesn't say anything at all. He walks around in silence, lost in thought, his eyes distant. When I talk to him I know he doesn't hear me; he's listening to something going on in his own mind.

Maybe it's his preoccupation with the sculpture; maybe it's Marsha. He has called her every night this week. He takes the phone into the hall and sits on the rug with his back against the wall. On nights when Mom and Dad are out late, he talks sometimes for hours. Richard complains that our line has rung busy for eight days in a row.

Tonight, from the living room, I hear Neeley's voice rising and falling as he talks to Marsha. The words are muffled, but his tone swings from tender to sharp. Then I hear the long silences and wonder what Marsha is saying to him.

Finally he hangs up the phone. His expression is strained, his jaw rigid. His eyes are rimmed with disappointment.

"How's Marsha?" I ask cautiously.

"OK."

"Then how come *you* don't look OK?"

He hunches his shoulders as if he is trying to ward off my questions.

I persist. "She just makes you unhappy. I don't know why you waste your time on her anyway."

Neeley looks at me with fiery eyes. "Don't worry, Holly, I won't be wasting my time much longer."

"What do you mean?"

His words erupt in a raw anguish. "Marsha . . . she wants to be free to date other guys."

I'm silent for a minute. Then gently I ask, "Will you see her again?"

Neeley stretches out in Dad's chair and thumps his fingertips on the nearby table. "She's going with me to the Easter Cantata tomorrow night."

"Well, that's something."

"Yeah, sure, something."

Mom arrives home then, her car rumbling up the driveway, and I sense that all talk of Marsha must end. Mom and Dad have no idea of the troubles Neeley's having with Marsha.

Mom comes in the door shaking rain off her umbrella. Her hair is wet; her mascara is smudged under her eyes. She looks at Neeley and me and shakes her head tiredly. "Don't ever let anyone talk you into showing a house twenty miles out in the country on a rainy day."

I go over and help Mom with her wet things. "What happened?"

"The subdivision is new, and the roads aren't paved yet. I got stuck in the mud. Luckily a kind man gave me a push."

"Isn't that something, Neeley?" I ask, trying to draw him into the conversation. He's sitting slumped in the chair, his chin on his chest. He pretends to be dozing. I know he's not.

"Well, you kids had a nice cozy evening by the fire while your folks were out grubbing for a buck," Mom teases. When Neeley still doesn't rouse, she looks at me. "Did you find something for dinner, hon?"

"Frozen pizza. But it's all gone."

"That's OK. I grabbed a bite earlier. Everything OK here?"

"Sure. Fine."

"Neeley must have exhausted himself working on that sculpture of his," she muses.

"Yes, I guess so."

Mom looks worried. "I don't know why he can't let up a little," she laments. "It's only a school project."

"He wants it to be right, Mom."

"No, he wants it to be *perfect*." She starts down the hall to the bathroom. "I'm going to put this umbrella in the tub to dry. Holly, would you put the kettle on? I'm dying for a cup of coffee."

"Sure, Mom."

She stops and gazes at me, looking almost apologetic. "I've got a big dinner planned for tomorrow, sweetheart. It'll be a nice family day with all of us together. We'll have fun, OK?"

There is something both sad and eager in Mom's expression. For an instant I feel sorry for her, as if she were the child and I the adult. It is a strange feeling. Then it's gone. I go over and quickly brush her cheek with a kiss. "Tomorrow sounds terrific, Mom," I assure her.

7

Somehow we make it to the Easter sunrise service. It isn't easy. Dad is frustrated because we didn't get an early start; Mom is peeved because everyone gobbled breakfast on the run; Neeley cut himself shaving and is threatening now to grow a beard. And I slept on my hair wrong and now it sticks out in funny little bunches. Plus, I ran my new panty hose climbing into the car.

Now we are sitting on hard folding chairs, the last row, in the church parking lot, watching a pale sun make its unhurried appearance on the horizon. The sky is overcast, the air bone-chilling damp.

I am trying to concentrate on what Pastor Collins is saying. I feel guilty because it is Easter morning and I don't feel the least bit spiritual. I want to think about Jesus and all the wonderful things He did for me, but everything else is crowding in.

Pastor Collins is talking about how Jesus died on the cross for our sins and rose from the dead so someday we can live forever in heaven with Him. I know the story by heart. When I was five I asked Jesus into my life at vacation Bible school. Neeley accepted Jesus as his Savior that same year. He was eight. Mom and Dad have been Christians for as long as I can remember.

We go to church every Sunday. We say grace at meals. I pray and read my Bible sometimes. But not often. Now, this Easter morning, I close my eyes and silently resolve, *I'll try to do better, Lord Jesus.*''

By the time the choir sings the "Hallelujah Chorus," I feel warm and happy inside. I wish I could feel this way all the time. I want to love Jesus and serve Him. I want to be the best Christian I can be.

But by the time church and Sunday school are over and we're on our way home, the good feeling is gone. Mom and Dad are still out of sorts, and Neeley is sullen. Everything is crowding in again, pushing Jesus out. In my mind I promise to pray tonight before I go to bed. Maybe the peaceful feeling will come back.

Mom fixes a delicious Easter dinner—baked ham, scalloped potatoes, yams, and fresh fruit salad. But the food is better than our conversation. Mom and Dad haven't seem much of each other this past week, and they blame each other.

Dad says, "When you took this job in real estate, Marge, I assumed it was part time. But lately you're gone more evenings than I am."

Mom replies, "When people want to see houses I have to be available."

"You have too many evening appointments."

"People work during the day," explains Mom.

"The kids need you here at home," argues Dad.

"Well, where have *you* been all these years?" counters Mom.

"Out day and night selling insurance, so we can eat—not to mention enjoy a hundred other necessities!"

"I know," Mom replies coolly. "That's why I'm working too."

"It's this lousy economy," complains Dad. Worry lines furrow deep in his forehead. "With prices so high, I don't know how kids today can make it." He looks over at Neeley. "You listening, son?"

Neeley looks up blankly. "What, Dad?"

Dad heaves a disgruntled sigh. "Sometimes I think you live in a dream world, Neeley. You have no idea what the real world is all about."

"I know my own world," says Neeley thickly. "That's good enough for me."

"That won't cut it when you're out on your own with no one else to foot the bills." Dad's voice rises a notch. "You kids today take it for granted there'll always be someone around to dole out the cash. Well, you'd better wake up, because even Uncle Sam is going broke."

Mom reaches over and pats Dad's arm. "Stewart, this is Easter, our special family day, remember? Can't we keep things light?"

Dad manages a contrite grimace. "I'm sorry. It just frustrates me that we have to kill ourselves making a living. We should be spending more time together as a family."

"Neeley and I understand, Dad," I reply, figuring it's my turn to say something. "We appreciate how hard you and Mom work."

Dad's expression relaxes. He looks over at Neeley. "I'll tell you what, son. It's your birthday next weekend. How about if we take some time off and go hunting together? Just us men."

Neeley pokes at his salad. "You know how I feel about hunting, Dad."

"Neeley would rather sketch deer than shoot them," I offer.

"Nonsense," returns Dad. "A boy Neeley's age shouldn't be so sentimental. Come on, Neeley. Say you'll give it a try."

Neeley looks up with troubled eyes. "I can't, Dad."

"Why not?"

"I've got to work on my sculpture next weekend."

"Every time I see you, you're working on that thing. How long do you have to spend on it?"

"I don't know. Until it's done."

"Are you neglecting your other studies?"

Neeley looks away.

"I asked you a question, son."

"I'm doing OK, Dad."

"I hope so. You have less than two months to make those grades for college. Don't slip up now."

"I'll get by," snaps Neeley.

"Then don't waste all your time in your room on that piece of clay."

Neeley stresses each syllable. "I'm not wasting my time, Dad."

"All right, *waste* is the wrong word. You know what I mean."

Neeley looks urgently at Dad. "It's not just a piece of clay. Don't you understand? It's important to me."

"That's what I mean about your sense of reality, Neeley." Dad's tone is stern. "It's just *one* project for *one* class. You've got to keep it in proper perspective."

Neeley's shoulders sag. "Yes sir."

Mom pushes back her chair and stands abruptly. Dad looks at her and asks, "Where are you going, Marge?"

"To get my medicine. I have a tension headache."

"You take too many of those antidepressants."

"I know I do. When the pressures let up, I'll get rid of them."

Dad glances at his watch and says brusquely, "If we're going to make it to the cantata tonight, we'd better get ready."

"Are you riding with us, Neeley?" asks Mom as she opens her medicine bottle and empties a tablet into her palm.

Neeley crumples his napkin, tosses it on the table, and stands up. "No. I'll drive. I'm taking Marsha."

"Oh, that's nice," replies Mom. She swallows her pill, then says with forced cheerfulness, "Why don't you bring her over afterward for dessert? I baked two lemon pies just for today."

Neeley gives Mom a long, wistful look. "Thanks, I'll ask her," he says. Then, in an impulsive gesture, he goes over and hugs Mom briefly, turns, and walks out of the room.

8

Marsha Piper is standing in our doorway looking as if she just stepped off the cover of *Seventeen* magazine. Her black, stylish hair accentuates a peaches-and-cream complexion; her eyelashes are thick with mascara; and her arched brows are penciled in with a delicate precision. She is gorgeous. I could barf.

"Hi, Marsha," I say, pretending cordiality.

"Hello, Holly," she returns loftily as Neeley shows her into the living room.

"I love your outfit," I bubble. "You always look so—so glamorous."

"Why, thank you, Holly." Her voice oozes like honey, but her words drop like buckets of cement: "And you always look so—so freshly scrubbed."

"It must be the Noxzema," I mumble and turn away. I can't win. Marsha is only two grades ahead of me, but the minute I step into her presence I'm reduced to a blabbering dunce. I feel as if my lipstick is smeared or I have spinach stuck in my braces or a hundred zits on my face.

We file into the kitchen where Mom is placing shimmering slices of lemon meringue pie on the table. Marsha sits down as if she is Princess Diana being seated by Prince Charles. She looks at Mom and gushes, "Thank you for inviting me over, Mrs. Rhoades. Your kitchen is so quaint and cozy. I just love it."

"Thank you, Marsha," says Mom as she pours us glasses of milk. "Did you enjoy the cantata?"

"Yes, it was very nice," replies Marsha in the silky voice she reserves for adults she wants to impress.

"I hope your parents didn't mind our taking you away from your own church this evening."

"Oh, no, Mrs. Rhoades. My folks play golf and take a lot of weekend trips. They're not much into religion."

"Well, then I'm glad you could join us."

Marsha turns to Neeley and coos, "Now that I'm here at your house I want to see that mysterious sculpture of yours."

I perk up instantly. "Oh, no one has seen it yet, Marsha. Not even me."

"Come on, Neeley. You're going to let me take one little peek, aren't you?"

"It's not finished," he says curtly.

Marsha's red lips form the slightest hint of a pout. "I don't care, Neeley. I want to see it."

"All right."

"All right?" I repeat, dumbfounded.

"Just remember it's not done yet," he cautions.

"If she can see it, I get to see it too," I insist, crossing my arms for emphasis.

Neeley chuckles. "You got it, half-pint."

After dessert, I follow Neeley and Marsha upstairs to his room. Butterflies mix with the pie in my stomach. I sense that this is an important unveiling. I find myself praying, *Please, Lord, let Marsha be crazy about Neeley's sculpture.*

We enter Neeley's room with its heavy, masculine furniture and plain brown bedspread and drapes. One wall is papered with half-finished sketches and reprints of famous paintings. On the opposite wall are several vivid watercolors Neeley painted of heaven. Several feet away, hanging alone, is Neeley's gloomy charcoal drawing of a hunter with his trophy—a huge, glassy-eyed buck.

In the corner by the window sits Neeley's easel with a three-way mirror crudely attached. Beside the easel is a small table supporting the sculpture. A white sheet covers Neeley's creation.

Marsha approaches gingerly. "Oh, my goodness, Neeley. It looks like a shroud."

He carefully removes the sheet, explaining, "A wet cloth keeps the clay moist and pliable."

Marsha and I both steal closer and inspect the life-size sculpture. It amazes me to see Neeley's likeness stamped in a mass of gray clay.

"It—it's perfect, Neeley," I murmur approvingly.

"Why, Neeley, it's just the cutest thing," trills Marsha. "Imagine you making this all by yourself. You're just absolutely clever."

Neeley seems to be addressing me as he explains solemnly, "It's not quite right, you see? I'm having trouble with the eyes. I've worked and worked on them, but they're still wrong. They belong to somebody else, not me."

"It doesn't matter, Neeley," I assure him. "This is wonderful. You should be proud."

"I'll be proud when it's right," Neeley replies.

Marsha has already turned from the sculpture to Neeley's stereo system. She eagerly flips through his cassette tapes, selects one, and sticks it in. "I hope you don't mind a little music, Neeley. I love good music, don't you?"

Silently Neeley replaces the sheet on his sculpture, arranging it just so. I decide it's time for me to make my exit, so I politely excuse myself and return downstairs.

Somehow I feel disappointed—and lonely. I wanted to stay and talk with Neeley about his sculpture. But Marsha was there. Marsha, always the intruder.

"She doesn't appreciate his work," I mutter to myself as I trudge to the kitchen. "She called his portrait *cute*. Doesn't she know *cute* is an insult to a real artist?"

Mom looks up from clearing the table. "Were you speaking to me, Holly?"

"No, Mom. Just talking to myself."

"Where are Neeley and Marsha?"

"Upstairs. Playing his latest tapes."

Mom looks thoughtful. "Holly, would you go back up and casually suggest that Neeley entertain Marsha down here?"

"Why? They're not doing anything wrong."

Mom gives me her exasperated look. "Holly!"

36

"OK, Mom, I'm going. Just save me an extra piece of pie."

I slink dutifully upstairs to Neeley's room. The door is half closed. Before I can enter I spot Neeley and Marsha in an embrace. He is kissing her passionately. I step back, surprised, embarrassed. I hear Neeley say, "I love you, Marsha. I'm nothing without you."

There is a scuffling sound, then Marsha says sharply, "Stop it, Neeley. I told you we can't be so serious."

Neeley's voice breaks with emotion. "I can't help it, Marsha. You make me crazy."

"See what I mean about you, Neeley?" Marsha counters. "You're too intense. You take everything so seriously. Why can't you just have fun and play the field like other guys do?"

"Yeah, I bet you know all about other guys!" snarls Neeley.

"There you go again—acting so possessive. I told you, I'm not your girl or anybody else's. I just want to have a good time with lots of people."

"Lots of *guys*, you mean."

"All right, lots of guys. What's wrong with that? I'm only sixteen, Neeley. I'm not about to settle down—or be *tied* down."

"Hon, it wouldn't be that way. I promise."

Marsha's voice sounds weary. Her syrupy facade is gone. "We've been through this before, Neeley. Listen, I like you. You're different from anyone I've ever known. You're talented and sincere and genuine—"

"Then you do still love me?"

"Wait. Let me finish. I see now that you're *too* different, Neeley. Too serious, too insecure. I can't handle it. I just can't. I—I really don't think we should see each other anymore."

Quietly I steal away from Neeley's door. I pray that he and Marsha won't hear me slip back downstairs. The last thing I hear is Neeley's desperate declaration, "Don't you understand, Marsha? I can't live without you!"

9

Monday morning. Neeley and I are late for school. He oversleeps. At 8:15 he comes bounding down the stairs two at a time, his shirttail flapping, his shoes in his hand. I wait while he plunders the laundry basket for matching socks, grabs an apple, and blows Mom a goodbye kiss.

We race each other to his Chevy, jump in, and peel out into the street like bandits making their getaway. While Neeley drives, I think about Marsha and last night, but I'm smart enough to keep my mouth shut about what I overheard.

Finally Neeley breaks the silence with, "You'll probably get a demerit for being tardy this morning."

"So will you."

"You didn't have to wait for me."

"I wanted to see how you were feeling."

"Checking up on me?"

"Why not? You're my number one brother."

"Your *only* brother."

"I rest my case." I look over at Neeley and study his features—his straight nose, strong chin, and high cheekbones. Any girl would love that face. Why doesn't Marsha? Cautiously I ask, "How come you overslept?"

"I was up late."

"*I'm* usually the night owl. *You're* the early bird."

"I couldn't sleep."

"How come?"

"What is this—twenty questions?"

"You've got circles under your eyes."

Neeley glances at me. "You don't look so hot yourself."

"Why not?"

"Too much lip gloss."

"I do not."

"You look like you just ate greasy pork chops—with no hands!"

I punch Neeley's arm. "At least you sound like the *old* Neeley."

He manages a grin. "You mean there's more than one of me?"

"A dozen at least. Take your pick."

He grimaces. "Do you think if I had any choice I'd pick *me*?"

"I would. Most of the time anyway."

"Don't do me any favors."

"I'm not," I insist. "You're OK, Neeley. Really. It's just that sometimes you're you—cheerful and fun, and other times lately you're this stranger—all gloomy and withdrawn."

Neeley's jaw juts forward as he shifts gears. "So what's the matter?" he quizzes. "You don't like the strong, silent type?"

"Only in the movies. At home I prefer my usual teasing, pesky brother."

"Maybe he's gone, Holly. Cured by an overdose of reality."

"Are you talking about Marsha?" I venture.

"You got it." He hesitates. "I've got other stuff on my mind too."

"What stuff?"

"Just stuff. When you're almost eighteen you start feeling the pressures—you know, life pushing in on all sides." He winks, as if he has made a joke.

"I'm not sure what you mean," I confess.

"Life," he repeats. "It's like being in a box that's closing in."

"That doesn't make any sense."

"You want me to draw you a picture? OK." Neeley's voice grows uneven, strained. "Imagine you're in a casket and it's dark and you can't breathe, and it's shrinking around you, getting tighter, you know, like it's going to snuff you out."

"That's gross," I say in disgust.

"Yeah? Well, I feel that way sometimes, Holly. Like I'm helpless. I keep trying, but I can't beat my way out of this blasted box."

I shift my books in my lap and look out the window. I don't like Neeley when he's like this. "Weird," I mumble under my breath.

"Well, you asked what was on my mind," he says defensively.

"I'm sorry I did."

"I'm sorry I told you."

I stare ahead through the windshield. Jefferson High School is just around the corner now—a big, two-story brick building—in what the kids call early-depression-style architecture. I'm determined to add a positive note before Neeley and I go our separate ways. I say brightly, "When you're eighteen you're supposed to have all the answers."

Neeley smiles grimly. "Then I've got until Friday to find them."

I decide to ignore Neeley's pessimism. "What are you going to do for your birthday?" I ask.

"Nothing special."

"But it has to be special. You'll be eighteen."

"I asked Marsha over, but she doesn't know if she can make it."

"Tell her Mom's planning to bake a luscious chocolate marshmallow cake."

Neeley pulls to a stop in the student parking lot. "You tell her, OK?"

"Sure, if I see her," I reply without enthusiasm. The idea of trying to convince Marsha to see Neeley doesn't appeal to me at all. As I reach for the door handle, I add, "Don't wait for me after school. I have Spanish club."

By the time I finish with Spanish club and trudge home with an armload of books, it's nearly 4:00 P.M. I knock on the door with my elbow, but no one answers. So I drop my books by the door and fish in my purse—the bottomless pit—for my house key.

I hate entering an empty house. It's the loneliest feeling in the world. I go in, drop my books in the nearest chair, and head for the kitchen. As I pass the den, I stop, surprised. Neeley is there, sitting on the sofa, with Dad's rifle lying across his knees. His head is cocked to one side as if he is listening to something. His eyes are fixed on some invisible point in space.

"Neeley?" I say tentatively. He doesn't hear me. "Neeley!"

He turns sharply, nearly dropping the rifle, and stares at me with an expression of shame, as if I have caught him doing something wrong. "Holly, you startled me."

I walk over and sit down across from him. "What are you doing with Dad's rifle?"

"Nothing. Just thinking."

"Thinking what?"

"Nothing—it doesn't matter."

"You never touch Dad's guns. You don't like guns."

"I know." He gets a peculiar look on his face. "I just wondered how it would feel in my hands, and—" His voice trails off.

"And what?"

He looks away and mumbles, "And whether I'd have the courage to use it."

"You mean go hunting?" I ask, amazed. "You told Dad you wouldn't go. You know you hate killing things."

"Not things. *Me.*" A crooked smile plays on his lips. His eyes don't quite meet mine.

I feel icicles go all the way down to my toes. Words are stuck like cotton in my throat, but I manage to expel them. "Neeley Rhoades, don't you ever say anything like that again. That's terrible—it's—it's sacreligious!"

He laughs, not his usual easy laugh, but a hard, hollow sound. "I'm only kidding, Holly. Can't you tell when a guy's making a joke?"

"It's no joke when it makes me feel like someone punched me in the stomach."

He stands up and puts the rifle back in the glass cabinet on the wall. Then he gives me a quick, contrite hug. "Don't tell

Dad I was messing around with his guns, OK, sis? He'd never stop pestering me to go out and bag some jackrabbit or deer."

"Deal," I say shakily. "Just stay out of the gun cabinet, OK? Those things give me the creeps."

He nods, but his voice is remote. "Don't worry, Holly. They leave me cold too." Then, without a backward glance, he saunters out of the room toward the stairs.

I watch him go. My feet refuse to move. My breath catches in my chest. At the edge of my consciousness perches a terror that has no name, no face, and no form. But I feel it just the same.

10

Today is Friday, Neeley's eighteenth birthday. Lori and I rush home from school to decorate the house with red and green streamers and bright balloons. Laughing like kindergartners, we wrap each other in crepe paper, like mummies. And we grow dizzy and giddy from blowing up too many balloons. In the kitchen we put a party favor and fancy paper hat beside each place setting and help Mom decorate Neeley's birthday cake with M & M's and yellow wax candles. Over the door we hang a sign that declares, "Happy Birthday to the World's Best Brother!" I vow this will be a day Neeley will always remember.

Lori leaves before Neeley gets home. She says she doesn't want to intrude on our family celebration, but I know she would love to stay. "Come back for dessert," I insist.

When Neeley finally walks in the door, only Mom and I are here to greet him. "Dad must have got tied up with a client," she offers lamely. I can tell she's angry.

We take turns giving Neeley a birthday hug. Then I take his hand and proudly show him all our festive handiwork.

"It's great, but you didn't have to go to all this trouble," he says, batting at a yellow balloon over the doorway.

"I wanted to do it," I assert. "I want this to be your best birthday ever."

Mom holds off dinner an extra half hour, hoping Dad will show. Neeley and I occupy ourselves with trying on paper hats and sneaking bites of frosting.

"So Marsha couldn't come?" I venture finally in my confidential voice.

Neeley's brow furrows. "No. She said she's grounded for the weekend. She failed a history test."

"That's too bad."

"Yeah." Neeley looks away, his signal that he doesn't want to talk about Marsha.

At last Mom serves dinner—roast beef, mashed potatoes, mushroom gravy, and creamed cauliflower. Neeley's favorite meal.

"We'll say grace when your dad gets here," she says evenly. The three of us eat in silence. It's not like I planned. Where's the joy and excitement?

Within minutes we hear the door open, and Dad walks in, looking harried and apologetic. "I tried my best to get away from that client," he explains, tossing his suit coat on a chair and loosening his tie.

"We just started a few minutes ago," Mom replies in her pleasant voice. She's trying her hardest not to make waves for Neeley's sake. Dad seems relieved. He sits down and helps himself to the roast beef. I recall that we haven't prayed yet, but somehow now it doesn't seem to fit, so I say nothing.

"So what are your big plans for tonight?" Dad asks Neeley.

"I'm going to work on my sculpture."

"No big date tonight?"

"No sir."

"Well, when is your art project due?"

"Monday."

"You'll be finished by then, won't you?"

"I don't think so."

"Why not?"

"I can't get the likeness just right. I keep trying, but it's not there."

"Well, you'd better turn it in as is. Your art teacher will understand."

Neeley grinds his jaw slightly. "I won't turn it in until it's right, Dad."

"Well, I can't imagine you allowing your stubbornness to jeopardize your grades, Neeley."

"You still have the whole weekend to get it right," I offer encouragingly.

The doorbell rings. Our conversation stops abruptly. Neeley jumps up and takes long strides to the door. "I bet Marsha found a way to come over after all," he reasons, his excitement evident.

But seconds later he returns with Lori. Disappointment is etched on his face, but he manages a fairly buoyant, "Look who just dropped by for dessert."

Lori hands Neeley a present wrapped with a large red ribbon. "I hope you like it," she says, her face flushing as she sits down beside him at the table.

I watch her gazing adoringly at him as he opens the package. *Why couldn't he like Lori instead of Marsha?* I wonder. *Things would be so much simpler!*

"Thanks, Lori," says Neeley as he holds up a sketch pad and a package of charcoal pencils. "I can sure use these."

"That's what I figured," she murmurs, pleased.

Impulsively Neeley leans over and kisses Lori's cheek—the sort of brotherly kiss he gives me. But I can tell Lori is dazzled.

Dad sits back in his chair and smiles approvingly at Neeley. "Well, son, now that you're eighteen, how does it feel to be a man?"

Neeley is silent. Did he hear Dad or is he just ignoring the question? But just as I am about to nudge Neeley, he replies vaguely, "I don't know what to say, Dad. Right now I honestly don't feel like anybody."

Dad looks mildly displeased by Neeley's response, but before he can say anything, Mom approaches the table with the birthday cake. "Everybody ready for this?" she asks brightly.

Neeley shakes his head. *He's not ready.* There is something restless and unsettled about him tonight, as if he is not really here with us at all. "Listen, Mom," he begins, tapping his fingers nervously on the table, "I'm going to call Marsha's parents and ask if she can come over just for cake and ice cream."

"But I thought she was grounded," Mom reminds him.

"I know, but maybe they don't realize this is a special occasion."

Neeley's words trail off as he goes to the wall phone and dials. "Hello, Mrs. Piper?" he begins, his voice formal and tense. "This is Neeley Rhoades. Yes, I'm fine, thank you. I—I'm sorry to bother you—I mean, I know Marsha is grounded, but today's my birthday and I—what? She's not home?"

Neeley shifts from one foot to the other. He is standing facing the wall so that we can't see his expression. We all sit in silence around the table, waiting, pretending not to listen but listening anyway.

"There must be some mistake, Mrs. Piper," Neeley maintains, sounding increasingly agitated. "Marsha wouldn't be out with somebody else. If she wasn't grounded, she'd be with me tonight."

He pauses, breathing hard. "She said she flunked her history test. She said that's why she couldn't come over."

Suddenly Neeley hits the wall hard with the flat of his hand. "What do you mean, she's going steady with David Higgins? That's crazy. When—when did that happen?"

Neeley's shoulders slump. His voice fills with resignation. "No, it's just that I hadn't heard. I mean, I didn't—she didn't mention it to me."

Neeley looks as if he is about to fold up. He teeters like a soldier wounded in battle. I want to run to him and cry with him, but his humiliation is already immense. I don't dare add to it by offering pity.

"Light the candles, Mom," I suggest as Neeley hangs up the phone. By the time he sits back down in his chair, his eyes dry and stunned, the cake is shimmering with a glow of eighteen tiny flames. We all launch into a shaky rendition of "Happy Birthday to You!"

Neeley manages a twisted smile and, with enormous effort, quips, "Just don't try out for the talent show at school, you guys."

"Make a wish, and blow out the candles, Neeley," I urge.

"I've used all my wishes," he utters under his breath, but he sucks in and blows anyway. Two candles remain lit. He looks at us and shrugs. "What do you know? I can't even blow out all my candles."

Mom serves the cake and ice cream with an air of forced frivolity. We all make an effort to keep things light and cheerful for Neeley. When we have finished dessert, Mom brings out a letter and hands it to Neeley. "This came today, honey," she explains, her voice hesitant. "If it's good news it will be a wonderful birthday gift. If it's bad news I saved it until now so it wouldn't spoil your party."

Neeley turns the envelope over in his hands, staring at it in disbelief. "It's from the Art Institute. They finally responded."

"Open it, Neeley," I press excitedly.

His expression grows animated. "You know, this letter could hold my whole future. If they accepted me, it'll mean everything I've ever dreamed of—"

"Marsha Piper, eat your heart out!" I bubble.

"Open it!" cries Lori.

Neeley tears open the envelope and removes a typewritten letter. He scans it eagerly. I wait, hardly daring to breathe.

Before Neeley says a word, I know the answer. His expression plummets. He blinks several times. His jaw grows rigid.

I expect him to explode, to pound the table, to spew out a torrent of angry words. But he carefully replaces the letter in its envelope, folds it, and tucks it in his shirt pocket.

"I'm sorry, Neeley," Mom says quietly. "I had so hoped. . . ."

Dad reaches over and squeezes Neeley's shoulder. "It's not the end of the world, son. Maybe this is a sign you should think along more practical lines. Tell you what. You and I'll sit down one of these days and check out the community colleges and state universities, OK?"

"Don't forget, Neeley," I remind him, "there's one more art school you haven't heard from yet."

"It's OK, Holly," he assures me. "I expected this. I really did."

"You mean you're not disappointed?"

"I feel OK, really." He stands up and smiles. He seems calm, almost relaxed. "Thank you all for a wonderful birthday."

He leans over and kisses Mom on the cheek, then me. "I love you all. You're wonderful."

"So are you, Neeley," I tell him earnestly. "And just wait. Next year's going to be your best birthday ever."

"You got it." He turns toward the door. "I'd better get to work on my sculpture if I'm going to turn it in on Monday."

After Neeley goes upstairs, Lori and I help Mom clean up the kitchen and do the dishes. Then we take down the streamers and balloons. We do a slapstick duet of "The Party's Over," until Dad teasingly threatens to throw something at the alley cats screeching out back.

Lori leaves at ten. At eleven Mom and Dad watch the news on TV. I head for bed. As I approach my room, I notice a sliver of light under Neeley's door. *He's still working*, I muse silently. I decide to wish him "Happy Birthday" one last time. I knock lightly, but there's no reply. I call his name softly. Still no response. I turn the knob. The door opens. I step inside. "Neeley, are you still awake? Neeley?"

I stop and stare down in horror. Neeley lies sprawled on the floor beside the bed. His face is a ghastly ashen-gray. I don't think he's breathing.

I break into a scream that will echo in my head and my heart for all the years of my life.

11

Mom and Dad and I are sitting in the emergency waiting room at Hope Memorial Hospital. It's after midnight.

Behind the closed double doors the doctors are working on Neeley, pumping his stomach or whatever they do when someone takes an overdose of drugs. We found two bottles of Mom's antidepressant medicine on the floor beside Neeley. They were empty.

We followed the ambulance to the hospital. We didn't say anything. It was as if words would shatter what little self-control we had.

All the way I stared fixedly through the windshield at the revolving red globe on the ambulance. The siren wailed, filling the night with its hideous, haunting sound. I pressed my lips together until my mouth hurt to be sure it wasn't really me screaming.

Now we are waiting. Waiting for some word about Neeley. We are sitting on an orange vinyl couch in a room with pale yellow walls. The room is noisy. The antiseptic smells turn my stomach.

People come and go, their heels clickety-clacking on the tile —men in white uniforms, a stern-faced policeman, a nurse pushing a cart, a pregnant lady. I sit and watch them without really thinking about them. I think only of Neeley—his face, the sound of his voice, his walk, his touch, his laughter.

Neeley has to be OK.

I tell myself this is all a dream, that I am not really here but home in bed and Neeley is in the next room and tomorrow morning we will go to church like always and I'll say, "You'll never guess the nightmare I had about you last night. Must have been the rich cake, the excitement of the party—"

Neeley—Neeley, don't die!

"He'll be OK. I know he will," I whisper to Mom. She doesn't seem to hear me. Her eyes are wide and unblinking, focused somewhere in space. She keeps twisting her purse strap. Her knuckles are white.

"Who would have thought—who'd imagine he'd take my medication?" she murmurs.

"I told you to get rid of that stuff weeks ago," Dad flares. He stands up and paces toward the double doors. He glances up and down the hall as if looking for someone with answers. He goes to the information desk and speaks to the nurse. She shrugs and shakes her head.

Dad comes back and gazes at us. I've never seen his face so tired and strained. "There's nothing yet," he sighs.

"Why don't they tell us something?" Mom implores in a small, desperate voice.

Dad sits down and runs his fingers through his thinning hair. "The nurse says they're doing all they can."

"What does that mean?" Mom retorts. "It doesn't tell us he'll be OK."

"He will—he has to be," replies Dad, his voice raw with feeling.

Mom begins to weep. She dabs her eyes with a tissue and blows her nose. "How could he do this, Stewart? Why?"

"I don't know, Marge."

"He's always been such a good, dependable boy. He was happy. Wasn't he happy?"

"I thought so."

"Maybe it was bad influences at school—a wild crowd. Maybe they persuaded him to experiment with drugs—"

"No, Mom," I tell her. "Neeley never took drugs."

"Then why would he do this? It's insane!"

Before Dad or I can respond, the double doors swing open, and a doctor comes out. He pauses, then moves purposefully toward us. His thick brows shadow his eyes as he says, "Mr. and Mrs. Rhoades?"

Mom and Dad stand up. Dad's arm circles Mom's waist as he utters a single word. "Neeley?"

The doctor shakes his head.

I shut out the doctor. I shut out Mom and Dad. I don't want to be here. I don't want this to be happening. I tell myself, *Neeley's fine. We'll take him home now, good as new. After all, bad things happen to other people, terrible things, but they get through them, and things go back to normal. Neeley is alive, and I'll never take him for granted again.*

"I'm sorry," the doctor is saying.

No! Neeley can't be dead! Other people die—people in the newspaper, people on TV, even people in the same neighborhood. But not the ones in your own house, not the people you can't live without!

I am jerked back to reality by Mom's anguished cries. "Oh, no! No! Not Neeley!"

I stare at the doctor.

"It was too late," he says, lowering his gaze. "The effect of all that Amitriptyline on his heart—" He shrugs helplessly. "It caused severe cardiac arrhythmia—we just couldn't bring him back—"

I jump up in blind fury and hit this man—this unwelcome stranger—hard with my fists and shriek, "Give me back my brother!"

12

The kitchen is still brimming over with food—pies and cakes and casseroles and cookies, tins of homemade candy and loaves of freshly baked bread. More food than I've ever seen in our kitchen before. The house is filled with delicious aromas.

I catch myself thinking, *Neeley's going to love this luscious coffee cake and these yummy chocolate chip cookies*. Then my heart sinks as reality hits home.

Neeley is dead.

That's why we have all this stuff. That's why the neighbors and the church people came by all day long, bearing gifts—love offerings to go with the wordless hugs and tear-filled eyes. They brought gifts made with their hands to fill the stomach, knowing they couldn't bring Neeley back to fill the empty place in our hearts.

Today was the funeral. Tonight I walk from room to room staring at all the flowers and plants—bouquets of red roses with fancy ribbons, huge white and pink mums, and other flowers I never even knew existed.

There were too many bouquets to leave at the cemetery. Someone said, ''Take them home. Enjoy them.''

Now they sit on every table, giving the house a bizarre atmosphere of celebration. Their strong fragrances mix in the air with the kitchen aromas. The smells turn my stomach. I can't escape them. I will remember them forever like this. I will never like flowers again. I'll never again savor the fragrance of a rose.

I keep walking. I don't know why. I can't sit still. Maybe I'm afraid my thoughts will catch up with me. I go around and pick lint off the carpet and straighten chairs and rearrange the flowers. I want everything right, in order. I don't know why.

This afternoon the house swelled with people eating and talking, weeping and hugging. They filled up all the spaces. People I hadn't seen in months, or years, or ever. So many of Neeley's classmates swarmed over everything and left no room for dark thoughts or dangerous feelings.

But now they have all gone home. Now I'm alone and afraid to think, afraid to open my eyes, afraid to close them.

So I wander through the house and look at familiar things. I touch them—the lamps, the knickknacks, the sofa and chairs. I make sure they are there. I make sure they are real.

I want to make sure Mom and Dad are real too. I want to see them and touch them so they won't go away like Neeley. But they are upstairs. Their door is closed. The doctor was here. He gave Mom a shot to calm her nerves. I heard Dad ask in a hushed voice, "She's not going to have a nervous breakdown, is she?"

I wonder, *What do people do when they have a nervous breakdown? How do you know when you're having one?* Dad is worried about Mom. He watches her with narrow, anxious eyes. Does he think she'll take too many pills too?

I push away that possibility. It's an idea I can't tolerate.

I think instead about the funeral. My mind is drawn to it and repelled by it at the same time. I replay it in my thoughts like one of Richard's homemade video tapes. Lori and Richard sat with Mom and Dad and me in the family room, weeping along with us. Lori's eyes never left Neeley's closed casket. Lori's dad, Pastor Collins, his voice breaking with emotion, talked about Jesus being the resurrection and the life. I couldn't help thinking, *Jesus wasn't life for Neeley, or Neeley wouldn't be dead*.

Mr. Sawyer, the art teacher, stood up and said beautiful things about Neeley: "Neeley Rhoades might have been another Auguste Rodin." Silently I wondered where Mr. Sawyer's encouragement was when Neeley needed it.

One side of the church was filled with young people. Neeley's friends and classmates. Some weeping openly, others staring at the floor, their faces shadowed with disbelief.

After the service Marsha Piper came up to me, sobbing. For the first time ever her makeup was smudged. She looked like anybody else, like nobody. She drew me aside and said urgently, "I didn't mean to hurt him, Holly. You believe me, don't you? That's why I didn't tell him I was going steady. I never wanted to hurt him."

I turned away, but Marsha clutched my arm and cried, "It's not my fault, is it, Holly? He didn't do it because of me!"

Bitterly I replied, "What do you think?"

Now I feel guilty for treating Marsha so cruelly. But it is her fault, isn't it? Neeley's dead. It has to be somebody's fault!

I feel the tears coming again. Once they start I don't know how to stop them. I take a deep breath and concentrate instead on the pretty bowl of yellow chrysanthemums on the TV.

Neeley would love to paint those flowers.

You see, I'm doing it again. Neeley is connected with everything around me. I can't go through my life thinking of what Neeley would like or how he would react. But his roots are too deep in my mind and heart; they are tangled and growing together with my deepest feelings about myself. How can I disentangle him? How can I know where Neeley leaves off and I begin?

My thoughts are broken by the sound of a door opening upstairs. I hear Dad's voice calling down, "Holly, it's getting late. You need your rest."

"I'll be right up, Dad," I call back. "I'm just checking things."

"Don't be long."

"I won't. How's Mom?"

"She's asleep, finally."

"Good. Good night, Dad."

"Good night, Holly." His voice sounds so far away, so drained, so different.

I quickly wipe the wetness from my eyes with my shirt sleeve. Yes, it's nearly eleven. Time for bed.

It's strange to think of going about our usual routine without Neeley. How can anything ever be the same again? Yet I will go to bed and get up in the morning and dress and eat and do dishes and answer the phone and eat again and go to bed again and sleep. *Try* to sleep.

Maybe habit is easier than consciously thinking through new ways to behave or new things to do. The old ways are at least reassuring, safe, unthreatening.

So I walk through the house and turn out all the lights. I check the locks on the front door and back door. I make sure the burners are off on the stove. These are the usual duties of the last one to bed.

Duty. Habit. Routine. These are important words when everything inside you is numb.

I glance one last time around the living room. It looks empty and a little frightening now with only the moonlight streaming in the windows. A ray of light reflects across Neeley's senior portrait on the fireplace mantle. His image is shadowy, indistinct. I stand alone, shivering, gazing through darkness, surrounded by silence, staring at my brother's face. Suddenly I realize, with a wave of panic, why I have compulsively paced these rooms all evening.

I am looking for Neeley.

13

The doorbell rings a zillion times, so I go to open it, knowing Mom and Dad will never answer it. They're sequestered (Dad's word) in their room as usual and won't talk to anyone.

I open the door, gulping a deep breath, as if I'm afraid someone might be ready to hit me. I don't want to see anyone either, but whoever's outside is too persistent to go away.

It's Richard. I haven't seen him since Neeley's funeral. He stands on the porch looking a little sheepish and a whole lot ill at ease. He's got something under his arm—a videocassette, no doubt. His hair is slicked back in an unnatural way, not meandering over his forehead in its usual sheepdog style. And he's wearing his good shirt with the stiff collar. I can imagine his mom telling him, *If you're going to visit the Rhoades at a time like this, at least dress decently*. But then I remember it's Sunday and he's probably been to church.

"You been to church?" I ask as my way of greeting.

"Uh-huh."

"I figured. You're all dressed up."

"You like it?"

"I don't know. You look weird. Weirder than usual."

"It was my mom's idea—the hair. I used that smelly goop. It's awful."

"Yeah. It looks awful. Uh, I guess you wanna come in?" I ask, hoping he'll say no. Don't get me wrong. I like Richard a lot, but right now the idea of talking to anybody seems totally overwhelming.

"Right, I'd like to come in," Richard says, ducking inside. "The fewer people seeing me with this greasy kid stuff, the better."

"It's not that bad," I mumble, feeling a little anxious and irritated at once. Now that Richard's inside, I don't know what to do with him. Nothing is normal anymore, and I don't know how to make things normal again. Obviously, it was a mistake letting him in. Now how do I get him to go away?

"I missed you at church," he says matter-of-factly.

"We didn't go."

"I figured you wouldn't. I mean, I totally understand."

How can you understand? I want to shout. *How can anyone understand?* "We just couldn't face anyone yet," I explain lamely.

Before Richard can reply, I turn sharply and head for the kitchen. I walk swiftly, but he's right on my heels. It's strange. I don't want him looking me in the eye. Am I afraid of what he'll see in my face? Afraid he'll read how I'm feeling inside? Why should grief be so embarrassing?

"How are you feeling, Holly?" he asks, pulling back a chair.

So he hasn't read my eyes!

How do you think I'm feeling? I want to retort. *My brother just died, and I wish I were dead too!* But in a very small voice, I reply, "I'm numb."

"What? Numb?" We sit down, facing each other across the table.

"Yes. Numb." How many times does he want to hear it? Maybe he doesn't know what it means. *Numb*, as in without feeling . . . stunned . . . incredulous (one of my dollar words) . . . in shock.

"I still can't believe it happened," Richard murmurs. "I never knew anyone who died."

I can't bear the direction our conversation is going, so I ask abruptly, "Do you want something to eat?"

Richard looks at me in surprise, as if he hadn't expected me to think of food at a time like this.

"People keep bringing us casseroles and cakes and all kinds of stuff," I explain quickly. "We can't find places to put it all."

"Well, thanks, but I'm not hungry. We stopped for pizza after church."

"Oh." For some reason, going out for pizza sounds like an absolutely foreign thing to do anymore. I wonder, *When did I stop living on this planet and take up residence in another world, a terrible, timeless Twilight Zone? And is there any way back to Richard's world, any way to rewind the tape back to Neeley's birthday and make things come out another way?*

"I brought you something," says Richard tentatively, like he's not quite sure it's something I'll want, like he can't decide whether he's bringing me bad news or good news.

"What is it?" I ask, not really caring. Nothing Richard or anyone else brings me can make any difference now. Nothing can bring Neeley back. Nothing can take away this horrible numbness I feel inside.

"I thought you might want this." Richard hands me the videotape. "I didn't know if it was too soon," he says in his polite voice he usually reserves for teachers. "If it is, just stick it away somewhere, and forget it. But someday I think you'll be glad you have it."

I take the tape and turn it over in my hand, feigning curiosity. "I don't understand. What is it? This isn't when I rescued the cat in the tree, is it?"

"No. It's—" He pauses, and his face reddens a little, and for an instant I think he's going to grab the tape away from me and bolt out the door. "It's probably too soon," he says suddenly, pushing back his chair. "Maybe I should come back another time."

Like a lightning bolt, the truth dawns on me. The words come out in a hush. "It's Neeley, isn't it? A videotape of Neeley."

"Yeah. Last summer. When we went to the beach—you and Neeley and Lori and me. He taught you girls to swim and I taped it, remember?"

"I thought we confiscated that tape. Or made you promise to destroy it."

"You did—but I didn't. Now I figured—maybe you'd want it."

I thrust it back at Richard. "No, I don't want it. I don't ever want to see it."

He shrugs apologetically. "Sure, I understand. I'm sorry." He stands up and starts toward the door. "I'll call you, Holly . . . "

"No, Richard, wait!" I spring forward and grab the tape from his hands. "I—I do want it, Richard. I want to see it. Put it on now." Already I'm hurrying into the family room. I take the cassette from its case, slip it into the VCR, and turn on the TV.

Richard is right behind me. "Are you sure, Holly? Sure you want to see it now?"

"Yes, it's OK. See, I'm perfectly fine."

We sit down side by side on the sofa. I take the remote control device and fast forward, my eyes searching intently for Neeley. The picture flickers a moment, then I spot him. He is bending down on the beach, scooping up a handful of wet sand, pretending he's going to pitch it at the camera. Then he makes a silly grimace and rushes straight for the lens, until his face is so close it blocks out the light. I hear Neeley's voice: "How's that, Richard? A close-up! This close enough?"

Then Neeley backs up and grabs a laughing, embarrassed Lori in her neon-pink swimsuit, and twirls her around on the sand until they both stumble and collapse in a hilarious heap. "Hey, Richard," Neeley shouts gleefully, "is this an Oscar-winning performance, or what!"

I hear the sound of laughter. It's not on the tape. It's now, this moment. My voice. *I am laughing.*

Since the funeral I have been pinching myself to see if I'm really awake, to see if I can wake myself from this awful nightmare. But pinching has done no good. I can't feel the pinches. They don't tell me whether I'm awake or asleep, whether the nightmare is real or imaginary. I feel nothing. I am totally numb inside and out.

But now I'm laughing. Laughing at Neeley, at his antics. He so seldom let down his guard and had fun. He so rarely made a fool of himself or let himself go. But that day last summer at the beach—the day he taught Lori and me to swim—he was positively preposterous. Wonderfully zany. We all were. It was one of the best days of my life.

Richard and I are both laughing now. We watch ourselves on the TV screen, the four of us mocking the camera, mugging like monkeys making outrageous faces, pretending to walk like orangutans, then chasing one another through the water like the Three, er, *Four* Stooges.

"I can't believe it," I exclaim. "We were so crazy. We should have been locked up, carted off to the loony bin."

"We were in rare form," Richard agrees. He takes the remote control and fast forwards. "Wait'll you see this part, Holly, when Neeley was trying to teach Lori to float. She looks like a drowned rat, and the way Neeley was going with those swim lessons, I thought for sure that's how she was going to end up."

I feel nearly hypnotized watching my brother on tape—the oh, so familiar features and expressions and gestures. Neeley's face. Neeley's voice. Neeley here in this room. I knew it! It *was* just a nightmare. Neeley's not dead. He could never be dead. "Oh, Richard," I declare, stifling my laughter, "we've got to show this to Neeley."

And suddenly the spell is broken.

The icy numbness I've felt for days is gone—and the hurt floods in. A raw, open wound. I stare at the TV screen, at Neeley, big as life, coming in again for a close-up. Fiercely, I grab the remote control and hurl it at the television set, screaming, "Stop it, Neeley, stop it! You're dead! You're dead!"

Richard stares at me, and I stare back, stricken. I try to recover, to save face. "I mean, I *wish* we could have shown this tape to Neeley," I blurted stupidly. "I wish—I—"

But Richard knows the truth. He knows. I never believed Neeley was really gone—not when I was at the hospital, not even when I was at Neeley's funeral, not until—*now*. This instant!

In my mind, I am screaming with all my pent-up rage and horror, *Neeley is dead! My brother, Neeley, is dead!* But when I open my mouth to release the sound, the scream twists and knots in my throat, nearly stopping my breath. I suck frantically for air.

Richard shakes me. "Holly—Holly, are you OK?"

The tears wash up like a wave sweeping over me. I know they will explode and I will drown in the pain. Even as the sound of grief emerges from my throat, Richard gathers me into his arms and presses my head against his chest and holds me tight while the waves roll over me.

"I'm sorry, Holly," he says over and over. "It was a dumb thing showing you that tape. I'm so, so sorry."

I can't speak. My whole body shudders with sobs. I hold on to Richard like a drowning person clutching a rock. Only Richard is not a rock. He is warm and real and alive, and I want him to hold me like this forever.

Until the hurt goes away.

14

Today is what you might call an anniversary. No. Wrong word. Anniversary implies celebration. This is—I can't think of anything to call it. One month ago today Neeley died.

I think of him all the time. He's more important to me now than when he was alive. Absurd, isn't it? Irrational. A girl takes her older brother for granted. Like the furniture or the air, he's always there. You don't realize how much your life is tied up with him—until he's gone.

At school no one mentions Neeley. Even guys who were his friends don't talk to me. They turn and go the other way, pretending not to see me. It's OK. I don't need their politeness or their embarrassed stammerings. Besides, what can anybody say to a girl whose brother committed suicide?

I play this game. I'm too old for games, but I play it anyway. Every day when I walk home from school, I pretend Neeley is walking with me, shoulder to shoulder, mine lower than his. I hardly have to pretend, because I almost feel him there beside me.

In my mind I tell him things he should know—the nice things his art teacher said about him at the funeral, the way Marsha carried on, and how he finally did get an acceptance from an art school out of state, a week after he died. I tell Neeley all this and more on my way home from school.

I know this game is a weakness. I'm humoring myself, giving in to a ridiculous need. Because I can't talk to anyone at school. I can't talk to anyone at home either.

Mom is taking more pills than ever. Her face is awful. It has no expression. Did you ever try to talk to someone who has no expression, whose eyes are dead? I don't look at her now. At the dinner table, I stare past her, out the window, anywhere. But then none of us looks into each other's eyes anymore.

Now, when I walk home from school, talking in my head to Neeley, I ask, *What went wrong? Weren't you happy, Neeley? Weren't we enough for you? Wasn't God enough?* No, God wasn't enough for Neeley.

I cringe, thinking that. It's like blasphemy. The thought stuns me, stealing my breath. It's like a steel girder collapsing, demolishing the foundation of my faith.

We don't go to church anymore. Pastor Collins has stopped by and telephoned several times since the funeral, but Mom puts him off. "We have to recover," she tells him. "We can't face people yet."

Pastor Collins always says, "What better way to recover than with God's help? What better company than God's people?" His words don't reach Mom. She's stopped listening.

So have I. I think I know why. I don't trust God anymore. How can I trust Him when He took Neeley away? How can I trust Him with my own life? I want to hold on tight to what's left. What else might God snatch away?

I am scared. I used to talk to God; not often enough but sometimes. Now I talk to Neeley in the silence of my own head, and no one answers.

Today, as usual, these thoughts go on in my brain until I reach home. Then they click off. Dad is home early for a change, sitting in his chair, reading the newspaper, only not really reading, his face as vacant as mine. When he looks up past me, we exchange brief blanks of conversation. Then I thread my way to the kitchen and nod my head at Mom, who is busy at the stove. *Surprise, we're eating together for a meal!* I muse. Mom has fixed roast beef and creamed cauliflower—Neeley's favorites. He had them for his birthday dinner.

Mom's gaze is leaden. Benignly she says, "Holly, set the table, please."

Does she know what today is?

I am startled to see that I have laid out four plates and silverware without even realizing it. I scoop Neeley's place setting away quickly, but Mom has already noticed. Her gaze pierces me unmercifully.

It occurs to me that I'm becoming a robot, unthinking, unfeeling, performing necessary rituals of existence. The idea is unsettling, so hurriedly I force words from my mouth, pebbles of conversation tossed erratically at my mother. She looks my way, momentarily wary. I realize that I have sounded flippant, intrusive. I don't even recall what I said.

The three of us sit down to eat. Perfunctorily. Wordlessly. We don't say grace anymore. Utensils click noisily in the uneasy vacuum of silence. No one mentions Neeley. It is an unspoken rule. We have not mentioned Neeley's name since the funeral.

"Good dinner, Marge," remarks Dad.

"Thank you, Stewart."

My parents are impossibly polite. I grit my teeth against their painful formality, their refusal to say anything that is real. But then I am as adept at pretending as they. I wonder what Neeley would say—how hurt he would be—if he knew how swiftly his name has been banned from our speech, how completely his presence has been scoured from our lives. We are whitewashed, sterile, empty.

"How was school today, Holly?" My father is admirable in his effort to establish an atmosphere of normalcy.

"OK," I reply. I can recite my lines as flawlessly as they. "I have a term paper due next Thursday. Lori said I could borrow her typewriter."

"Good," says Dad, nodding. "Isn't that nice of her, Marge?"

Mom mumbles something in reply, words that seem garbled, inappropriate. The telephone rings, saving us all. I jump up to answer it. Then I sag slightly, recognizing Pastor Collins's voice.

"I just wanted you to know we're thinking of you," he offers, a gentle, sincere tone. "The last time I stopped by to see your folks, I missed you, Holly."

"Yeah, I know," I say uncomfortably. Then, feeling compelled to explain, to justify, I continue hastily, "We won't be there Sunday, not yet, not while things are still—I mean, we just can't—Mom already told you—"

Pastor Collins responds to my embarrassment. "I wasn't calling to check up on you, Holly. But if I can help—if there is anything I can do—anything I can say—"

"I don't know," I answer blankly. "What can you say?"

There is a pause, then Pastor Collins speaks up, his voice clear and persuasive. "I can say what's on my heart, Holly. And more important, I'd be happy to listen to what's on your heart. Perhaps I could come over, and we could talk sometime, have prayer together—"

"I don't know," I reply doubtfully, feeling cornered and yet aware of an unmistakable yearning inside. "I'd better go," I conclude. I don't add that Mom and Dad are watching me, their gaze mildly suspicious, skeptical.

"Very well, Holly. Give my regards to your folks. And Lori sends you her best. She hopes the two of you can get together soon. Please, let's all keep in touch, all right?"

"OK. Tell Lori I'll see her in school tomorrow. Goodbye." I hang up the receiver and sit down at the table, involuntarily sighing relief.

"Pastor Collins?" queries Dad, knowing very well who it was.

I nod. "He would like to see us again sometime, maybe have prayer together, he says."

"He's been by twice already," Dad snaps with irritation. "He should sense when people want to be left alone."

"I won't go back there," Mom insists. "I won't have people talking and staring—" She stops abruptly. She has stepped too close to threatening territory. She quickly turns her attention back to the food on her plate.

"Why don't you go ahead and say it, Mom?" I suggest, my voice trembling. "We have to face it sometime."

"What do you mean?" Mom asks coldly.

"Holly, this isn't the time," Dad interrupts, his tone almost brutal.

"Why not?" I demand, an unexpected geyser of emotion erupting inside me. Pockets of tears swell behind my eyes, but I persist. "What better time is there, Mom? We have to talk about Neeley sometime. Neeley—your son, my brother, remember? He killed himself. How can we keep trying to live like it never happened, like we never loved him? How can we go on acting like we died too?"

Mom looks as if she has been struck. When she finds her voice, she cries, "How dare you talk to me like that? Go to your room!"

"Marge, please," prompts Dad, pushing back his chair and standing.

"I'm going," I announce bitterly, "but don't tell me you don't think about Neeley. I've seen you go to his room every day and put a wet sheet over that clay head he was making. But what good will it do to keep the clay pliable if Neeley isn't here to finish it?"

Immediately Mom retreats within herself. I can see the physical change—the folding up of her personality, an orderly turning inward until the shell is secure. I am furious with myself for forcing the issue of Neeley. While Dad goes to comfort Mom, I escape up the stairs to my room.

No. I pause first at Neeley's door. It is always closed except when Mom goes in to change the sheet covering Neeley's sculpted head. Impulsively I go in, turn on the light and stare at all the things—books, art materials, drawings and paintings—that defined Neeley's life. They remain as he left them.

And of course, the clay bust—the self-portrait that Neeley couldn't get just right. I wonder, *Was he trying too hard, just as perhaps he was trying too hard to mold his own life, to do everything himself?* A peculiar idea.

Carefully I lift the damp sheet off the unfinished clay head. I recognize Neeley—the shape of his face, the long thin nose, the lean cheekbones, the solid jaw. But I see what Neeley must have seen. Something around the eyes are not quite right. They aren't Neeley's eyes. He tried so hard, but he didn't capture the eyes.

Why did he quit trying?

An anger rises in me sharply, verging on contempt. "Why did you do it, Neeley?" I say aloud. "Why, Neeley, why?"

My hand moves deftly, seemingly without my awareness. I have picked up a stylus from Neeley's desk. Savagely I plunge the pointed instrument into the mound of clay, the unfinished head. I draw back in shock. The clay has already hardened. The stylus fails to penetrate. "It didn't work, Mother," I shout. "It dried out, hard as a rock!"

I try again, stabbing vigorously, irrationally attacking the gray lifeless mass that taunts me with its resemblance to Neeley. Then I drop the stylus and pound on the clay with my fists, willing it to respond. It remains cold and hard, impenetrable.

"Holly!"

I turn dazedly and stare at Mom standing in the doorway with Dad. "You were screaming," Mom says apprehensively.

I cannot answer. In her face and Dad's I recognize my own overwhelming grief. My spirit feels lacerated, wrenched from its niche inside me. I flee to Mom, yielding to the sobs that surge through me like swiftly recurring quakes.

We exchange a brief, fierce embrace, shamelessly sharing our tears. Dad's arms stretch around us like protective wings.

"God, help us!" he whispers aloud.

I feel Dad's chest against me, heaving with sobs, and I wonder, *Will the vacuum of pain that envelops us ever fill with peace?*

15

"Hello, Holly? This is Lori. I'm calling to find out if you can spend Friday night with me."

"Friday night—at your house?" I feel a sudden panic in my chest.

"Sure, my house. Can you come?"

I hesitate, winding the telephone cord around my finger. I am trying to figure out how to turn Lori down without hurting her feelings.

"Holly, are you there? Please say you'll come. It's been ages since we've gotten together."

"I don't think so, Lori," I reply uneasily. "I haven't been out much since—you know. I think I should stick around the house."

"Do you want me to come over there?"

"No, you'd better not. Mom and Dad aren't up to company yet."

"*Company?* I'm your best friend, Holly."

"I know. But I just don't think I should have anyone over yet."

"Holly, it's been over a month. Don't you want to see me, you know, outside of school?"

"Sure I do. It's just that I—" Oh, no, I'm choking up! I'm going to bawl right here on the telephone.

"Holly, are you OK?"

"Yeah, I'm—I'm fine, Lori."

"You're not either. You're crying."

"No, I'm just—oh, this is stupid. I just feel weepy all of a sudden."

"I'm coming over, Holly. We can go for a walk or something. I'll be right there."

Fifteen minutes later Lori arrives. Her long, wheat-colored hair is windblown and tiny beads of sweat stand out on her nose.

"How'd you get here so fast?" I ask, showing her in.

"Rode my bike," she pants. "I forgot how many blocks it is to your house."

"Especially when you're trying to beat all speed records."

"I even steamed up my glasses." She laughs as she wipes the lenses with a tissue.

"Where do you want to go?" I ask.

"Not for a walk. I've had all the exercise I want for a while."

"I guess we could go to my room—if we're quiet."

Lori looks around. "Is someone home?"

"Yeah, Mom's in her room—sleeping."

"Oh, I figured she was out showing houses."

"I wish she was. She hasn't been back to the real estate office since . . . " I purposely let my words trail off.

"I'm sorry, Holly. I know it's been pretty rough for all of you."

I force a sound, something between a laugh and a cough. My lower lip is trembling. "It's been the pits." I paste on a smile and wave my hand breezily. "Some hostess I am, huh? You want a Coke or something?"

"No, let's just go up to your room."

We climb the stairs quietly, and I shut my door behind us. Lori and I sit on my bed and look at each other. I want to be cheerful and relaxed with Lori and say something clever, but there's a lump in my throat that keeps the words from coming.

"I've missed you at church, Holly," she says softly.

"Me too," I manage.

She pushes her glasses up on her nose. "You can cry if you want to."

"Oh, Lori," I begin. The floodgates open, and the rivers of anguish spill out. Lori and I sob together in each other's arms.

"I loved him too, Holly," she whispers.

I reach for the box of Kleenex on the bureau and offer it to Lori. We blow our noses and smile self-consciously.

"This time my glasses are really fogged," she says, taking another tissue.

I stand up and inspect my swollen eyes and red nose in the mirror. "I think you could safely say we have faces only a mother could love," I note solemnly.

"A mother orangutan, you mean." Lori peers blindly at her reflection. "Although, you know, without my glasses we don't look half bad."

"You're looking at Oscar, my stuffed, potbelly bear!" I tease.

"Good-looking dude," she replies, patting his round furry head.

We sit on the bed again and look at each other. "Thanks," I mumble.

"What for?"

"I don't know. For crying with me, I guess. It helps."

"Do you want to talk about it, Holly?"

I shrug.

"Do your folks say much?"

"No. In fact, they wouldn't even mention Neeley's name until last week." I cross my legs Indian-style. "I did this really crazy thing, Lori. I flipped out and started beating Neeley's sculpture. I was so angry—it was like a volcano erupting inside me. Mom and Dad came and held me, and we all cried. Now we talk about Neeley once in a while—safe, little things, you know?"

"Then maybe it was good you let out your feelings."

"I don't know. Before that I just felt numb. I couldn't believe Neeley was really gone." My voice cracks slightly. "Now the numbness has worn off, and there's this pain inside me. Sometimes it hurts so bad."

"Don't you think it'll get better with time?" Lori reasons.

I scowl. "Whoever said 'time heals all wounds' must have been talking about cuts and bruises and broken bones."

"But each day should get easier," Lori insists.

"You don't know anything about it!" I snap crossly.

Lori retreats. "But I'm trying to understand, Holly."

I reach over and squeeze Lori's arm. "I'm sorry. See what I mean? Everything's so unpredictable. I don't know how I'm going to feel, or what I'm going to say or do from one moment to the next." I sigh deeply, groping for words. "Sometimes I think I'm doing OK. Then something sets me off—maybe some dumb little thing—and I get depressed and feel so lousy."

"I wish I knew what to say, Holly."

"Just listening helps."

"That I can do—anytime."

I study the white half-moon on my index fingernail. "What bothers me too, Lori—I keep thinking about it—Neeley was so special. He was talented. He would have been a great artist. Sometimes I think it should have been me who died instead of him."

"You?" Lori looks shocked.

"Yes, me. Let's face it, Lori. I'm ordinary. I can't do anything special."

"You're special to me, Holly."

"That's because we're friends. But I won't ever be anybody great or famous, like Neeley would have been."

"Sure, Neeley was special, Holly, but so are you. It's true."

I push back the cuticle on my nail until it hurts. "I don't know what's true anymore, Lori. Lately I just feel all mixed up inside."

"Maybe you should talk to someone, Holly."

"I am. I'm talking to you. And I've talked some to Richard."

"I mean someone else."

"There isn't anybody. Besides, what good would it do? It won't bring Neeley back."

"I know. But you might get some answers."

I stand up abruptly and smooth out my jeans. "There aren't any answers, Lori."

"How about talking to my dad?"

"Get serious!"

"I am. He really wants to help, Holly."

"Well, he might be 'Dad' to you, Lori, but he's Pastor Collins to me. I wouldn't know what to say to him."

"Then just listen."

"No way."

"Would you spend Friday night at my house?"

"Why? So I can talk to your dad?"

"Not exactly. But if it just happened—"

"What is this, Lori? You think I need a shrink?"

She shakes her head slowly. "No, Holly, but I think you need someone to help you through the hurt."

16

I change my mind and go to Lori's house on Friday night after all. When she opens the door, I look beseechingly at her and exclaim, "Oh, Lori, I had to come! I hate being at home these days."

Lori welcomes me in and takes my overnight case while I rant on. "We go around like zombies, Lori. Dad works till all hours, and Mom lives on her pills. She sits and stares at the TV, but she doesn't see it. She doesn't even see me. I don't know how I'll stand it when I'm home for the entire summer."

Sadly Lori replies, "I've been praying so hard that things would get better."

"They won't ever get better," I reply bitterly. "Not without Neeley."

While I sit down on the sofa and catch my breath, Lori goes to the next room to talk with her mother. Minutes later Lori returns and announces, "Tonight we're going to have a good time, Holly. Mom's turning the kitchen over to us. We're making homemade chili and chocolate brownies."

"Uh oh, I forgot the Alka-Selzer," I reply, making a feeble stab at humor.

The evening goes just as Lori predicted. We have fun cooking and baking, more fun eating, not quite so much fun cleaning up the mess in the kitchen. It feels good to be with a normal family again. Lori's mother is her usual cheerful self. I don't even feel intimidated by Pastor Collins. Tonight, in his casual, rumpled clothes, eating brownies and milk, he's just Lori's father. He doesn't even make me feel guilty about missing church lately.

"How about a game of Scrabble?" he suggests after we've consumed our brownies.

"Aw, Dad, you always win," Lori reminds him.

"You girls can have the dictionary. I won't even touch it!"

"Well, in that case—" Lori looks questioningly at me.

"It beats staring at the boob tube," I reply.

We play for an hour. Pastor Collins wins as usual. He forms the words "zebra" across and "zone" down in a single play. "That's triple letter score for the Z," he adds with a hint of smugness.

"You did it again, Dad," says Lori accusingly.

He pushes his glasses up on his nose—Lori's favorite gesture. His brown eyes twinkle. "Why, you girls handed me that game."

"I couldn't concentrate," I admit.

"Just wait'll next time," warns Lori with a grin. She leans down and scoops up her fat, yellow cat, Macaroni. Everyone calls him Mac for short, which seems to suit him fine. He purrs contentedly and observes the world through narrow, aloof, green eyes.

"Let's go play with Mac," Lori suggests. I follow her to the living room. We sit on the plush gold rug by the fireplace and tease Mac with his squeaky rubber mouse.

Pastor Collins sits near us in his La-Z-Boy and reads his newspaper. After a few moments he puts down the paper and smiles at me. "Holly, I understand you'd like us to have a little talk sometime," he says kindly.

"A talk?" I echo, dumbfounded. I stare daggers at Lori, but she's conveniently busy with Mac.

Pastor Collins leans forward, folding his arms across his knees. "I imagine there aren't too many people who talk to you about Neeley."

I stare awkwardly at my hands. "No sir."

"He was very important to you, Holly. You need to be able to talk about him."

"Yes sir."

74

"Sometimes people want to help, but they don't know what you need to hear."

"Everybody pretends like Neeley never even existed," I reply. "That hurts most of all."

"Perhaps they don't want to bring up a painful subject, Holly. They don't realize Neeley's on your mind most of the time anyway."

"How did you know?" I ask in surprise.

Pastor Collins' expression softens. There is a faraway light in his eyes. "I had a sister who died when I was very young," he tells me, his voice catching slightly. "For a long time I felt very sad and guilty."

I stare up into Pastor Collins' face. "Why did you feel guilty?"

"Because I sometimes got angry with Annie when she played with my things. Once I said I wished she was dead. When she did die, I blamed myself."

I trace an imaginary circle on the carpet. "I feel guilty sometimes about Neeley," I murmur.

"Do you, Holly?" Pastor Collins' voice is very gentle. "Would you like to tell me about it?"

I keep my eyes on the rug, making my invisible circle larger and larger. "I keep thinking there must be something I could have done . . . something to stop him." I look up imploringly at Pastor Collins. "I should have known. I should have done something. I should have kept him from dying!"

Pastor Collins reaches over and puts his hand on my shoulder. "To do that, Holly, you would have to be God."

I feel the tears coming. I blink quickly to force them back. "Then why didn't God stop Neeley?"

Pastor Collins shakes his head. I expect a sermon now, but he says simply, "I don't know."

I look up, startled. "You don't know either?"

"No," he concedes, "but I'm satisfied that God has the answers. Someday we'll know them too."

"Someday isn't now."

"No, and it doesn't help the hurt now, does it?" He sits back in his chair, looking thoughtful. "Did you know, Holly, that I've struggled with guilt feelings over Neeley too?"

"You have? But why?"

"I was Neeley's pastor. He was part of our church family all of his life. And yet I never saw him as needy. I've wondered how I might have helped him, how I could have been more available to him."

"But it wasn't your fault."

"No, Holly, and it wasn't yours either. Nor was it your parents' fault, but I suspect they feel very guilty too."

"They don't say anything, but I know they feel bad." I look questioningly at Pastor Collins. "If it wasn't anyone's fault, then why did it happen?"

"I've asked myself that too, Holly. I don't know why it happened." Pastor Collins sits back and inhales deeply. But his eyes remain fixed on me. "Tell me, Holly, what troubles you the most?"

I look away. One question torments me over and over, but I'm afraid to say it out loud. Finally I meet his gaze. "I keep wondering—"

"What is it, Holly?"

The words tear from my throat. "I gotta know—is Neeley in heaven?"

For several moments Pastor Collins looks deep in thought. At last he says, "Tell me, didn't Neeley know Christ as his own personal Savior?"

"Yes, he accepted Jesus in Bible school when he was eight," I answer. "When I was little, Neeley helped me say my prayers. I know he loved Jesus."

"Well, if Neeley was truly God's child, committing suicide didn't change that fact."

"Then he is in heaven?" I persist.

Pastor Collins rubs his chin slowly. "God's Word promises something very special, Holly," he replies. "Let me paraphrase Ephesians two, eight and nine especially for Neeley. 'For by grace was Neeley saved through faith, and not of himself. It was the gift of God, not of works, lest Neeley would have boasted.' You see, Holly, God doesn't add the condition that a person is saved as long as he doesn't commit suicide."

I fight back tears. "I was so afraid that Neeley . . . " The idea is too repellent to put into words.

Pastor Collins smiles consolingly. "Holly, when Jesus died for our sins, He paid for all of them—those we've already committed, those we haven't even thought of yet, and yes, I believe even the sin of suicide."

"But it must have made God awful unhappy . . ."

"Yes, Neeley grieved Jesus deeply when he took his life out of God's hands. After all, God had a very special plan and purpose for Neeley's life. Neeley violated God's timetable and lost out on all the wonderful things God had in store for him. That's a great tragedy, and Neeley was terribly wrong to do such a thing. But remember, the Lord doesn't ask us to *deserve* salvation, only to *accept* it."

I can't hold back the tears any longer. I weep softly at first, then harder. An immense sense of relief sweeps over me as I imagine Neeley safe in heaven. Pastor Collins gives me his handkerchief, and Lori puts her arm around my shoulder. They sit in sympathetic silence for several minutes while I cry.

"I'm sorry for bawling," I say finally, between sniffs.

"Never apologize for crying, Holly," Pastor Collins tells me gently. "Tears help heal the hurt."

I work at a grateful smile. Mac the cat climbs into my lap and stretches lazily. I smooth his fur and scratch behind his ears. I realize crying made me feel better, but I'm still troubled by the *way* Neeley died. I glance up at Pastor Collins and bite my lip, struggling for words. "Neeley's the only one I've ever known who . . . committed suicide." The words stick in my throat. "There's so much I still don't understand."

17

"Holly, suicide is one of the leading causes of death among young people."

I look at him in disbelief.

"That's the sad truth." Pastor Collins gazes soberly at Lori, then at me. "That doesn't even count suicides that aren't reported as such. And for every suicide, there may be as many as fifty attempts daily."

I change positions on the rug, folding my legs against my chest and resting my chin on my knees. "I thought Neeley was the only one," I begin tentatively. "I mean, I never thought about it happening to other people."

"It happens every day, Holly," Pastor Collins replies.

My lower lip trembles. "But why do they do it?" I implore. "What made *Neeley* do it?"

Pastor Collins shakes his head. "I don't know what reasons Neeley had, Holly. A loss of some kind, a broken relationship."

Anger bristles under my skin as I retort, "I knew it was Marsha's fault!"

"Not necessarily, Holly. There are other reasons too. Broken homes, drug abuse, school failures, family crises, and feelings of rejection or inferiority. In fact, someone has said, 'Suicide is the severest form of self-criticism.'"

"What does that mean?" I ask.

"Well, people who consider suicide are often high achievers," explains Pastor Collins. "They set impossible standards for themselves and then suffer excessive guilt over their failures. They panic when they feel they're not in control of their own lives."

"That sounds like Neeley," I admit.

Lori looks thoughtful. "But Daddy, we all have problems. Why couldn't Neeley solve his problems?"

"Neeley's problems may have brought on depression, and his depression may have prevented him from solving his problems. It's a vicious circle."

"Well, I've been depressed sometimes," interjects Lori, "but I'd never kill myself."

"Me neither," I agree solemnly.

Pastor Collins nods. "The person considering suicide is often weighted down by feelings of helplessness, hopelessness, and loneliness. So, in a sense, he's not really trying to kill himself. He's killing the hopelessness."

"But Christians aren't supposed to be depressed, are they, Dad?"

Pastor Collins leans forward as if to tell us a secret. "Some of the greatest men in the Bible had times when they were so depressed they wanted to die."

Lori and I stare at each other. Together we exclaim, "Who?"

"Moses, for one, after he led the Israelite people out of the wilderness," notes Pastor Collins. "And Elijah, when he was pursued by wicked Queen Jezebel."

"Who else, Daddy?"

"Well, there was Job, who lost all his family and possessions. And remember that David wrote some of his most beautiful psalms when he was deeply depressed." Pastor Collins pauses contemplatively. "Even Jesus was sorrowful unto death when He prayed in the garden of Gethsemane before facing the cross."

"Does that mean being depressed is OK?" Lori asks.

He smiles. "I think a more relevant question is, What will our reaction be when depression strikes? Will we let it destroy us? Or will we recognize depression as a symptom of a need in our life, a need that requires greater reliance on God and a deeper relationship with Him?"

79

"What should we do when we feel depressed or angry or afraid?" I ask.

"Acknowledge the feeling, and turn it over to God," Pastor Collins replies. "Then do something positive—a physical activity like jogging, for example. You might sing one of your favorite choruses. Or do something involving other people, like talking to a friend or doing someone a favor."

"I always feel better when I talk to Lori or Richard," I acknowledge.

"That's good, Holly. Sharing your feelings with a close friend is one of the best ways to relieve depression."

I lean back on the rug and stretch my legs out in front of me. My mind is whirling, trying to understand all that Pastor Collins has said. A question still bothers me. "Isn't there some way to keep from getting depressed in the first place? Neeley felt bad about Marsha and his rejection from art school. I guess he figured the only way to make the bad feelings go away was to—to—" My voice breaks. I still can't talk about Neeley.

Pastor Collins picks up the conversation. "Holly, as Christians we can choose to look inward at ourselves or outward at Christ. If we become too self-absorbed, we may become conceited, thinking we're better than we are, or we might suffer an inferiority complex, thinking we're worse than we are. Either way, our eyes are on ourselves, not Christ."

Lori and I exchange meaningful glances. "You mean if we feel inferior, we're just as bad as—as someone like that stuck-up Marsha Piper?" I wonder aloud.

"Sometimes when I'm on my diet I'm pretty self-absorbed," Lori confesses. "I think about me eating lasagna, me eating banana splits, me eating chocolate cake—"

"When I got my braces, I wouldn't smile for weeks," I reveal reluctantly. "I figure everyone was calling me metal-mouth or tin-grin behind my back."

"And I'd rather be blind and bump into things than have people see me in my glasses. *Some* people anyway," admits Lori. "I guess that's as bad as Marsha always thinking how terrific she is."

"Not in my opinion," I remark emphatically.

Lori looks uncertain. "But, Daddy, are you saying we shouldn't think about ourselves at all?"

"Of course not, honey. After all, God created us in His image, and we're very special to Him." He pauses. "But if we have feelings of inferiority we need to realize that God is with us and ready to help us."

"And, boy, do I need help," muses Lori, pushing her glasses up on her nose.

"But remember, Lori," cautions Pastor Collins, "God doesn't want you to dwell on how *bad* you think you are. That would still be preoccupation with yourself. He wants your goal to be self-forgetfulness."

"I'm already forgetful," she notes.

Pastor Collins laughs lightly. "I don't mean absentmindedness, honey." He gestures toward the large Bible on the coffee table. "Do you recall the incident in Matthew when Christ walks on the water?"

Lori sits forward eagerly. "Peter wanted to get to Jesus so he jumped out of the boat and started walking on the water too."

"But then what happened?"

"Peter sank," I say quickly.

"Why?"

"Because he took his eyes off Jesus."

"That's right. He became fearful when he looked at himself and his circumstances. So he sank."

"He was afraid he would drown," I offer. "But Jesus saved him."

"That's true, Holly." Pastor Collins folds his hands across his ample middle. "The point is, when we turn inward and focus on ourselves, we tend to become fearful, bitter people. And if we're constantly fearful, eventually we may self-destruct."

I nod knowingly. "Neeley was afraid. He was afraid he couldn't be a great artist . . . and that Marsha wouldn't love him . . . and that he couldn't go to art school."

Lori gazes somberly into space. After a minute, she asks, "Daddy, if Neeley was a Christian, why didn't he let God help him?"

Lines of consternation settle in Pastor Collins' forehead. "I don't know, Lori," he says. "Sometimes when things go wrong, we feel as if God has abandoned us. It takes faith to seek Christ in the midst of difficult circumstances.''

"Sometimes it's even harder to seek Him when things are going OK," I offer.

"An astute observation, Holly," notes Pastor Collins with a twinkle. He sits forward and says intently, "Do you follow what I'm saying? When our focus is on Christ, we become more loving, giving, confident people. You see, fear inhibits us, but love releases us. Frees us. Love has nothing to lose, so we can go for it, just be ourselves." Pastor Collins gestures expansively. "And when we truly believe God loves, forgives, and accepts us, then we're free to love, forgive, and accept ourselves and others.''

Immediately I think of Marsha Piper. I could never love her! "Some people are easy to love, but others—yuck!''

Lori and her father both laugh. Then, more seriously, he replies, "Yes, Holly, we're fortunate that God doesn't ask us to have warm emotional feelings toward everyone. We simply couldn't.''

Lori looks perplexed. "But if love isn't how we feel, what is it, Daddy?''

"Well, the kind of love God talks about has little to do with our feelings, Lori. It's a conscious decision of our will to behave lovingly, to do the considerate, generous thing on behalf of another person. Real love costs us something, some effort. Jesus chose to love us when we were unlovable, and it cost Him His life.''

I lower my gaze and confess reluctantly, "Sometimes I don't love God very much. I'm still angry at Him because He took Neeley away.''

Pastor Collins extends his hand and squeezes my shoulder again. His voice is warm and gentle. "Like I said, Holly, love isn't just a matter of feelings. Love is you staking your life on Christ. It's you deciding to make Him your first priority, no matter what. It's you trusting Him even when nothing around you makes sense. It's that kind of love that casts out our fears and makes us free inside.''

Tears swim in my eyes. "I wish Neeley hadn't been afraid," I sob. "I wish he could have been happy.''

Pastor Collins leans down and looks me in the eyes. "It wasn't happiness he needed, Holly. Happiness comes and goes with our circumstances. It was *joy*."

"Joy?"

"Yes, Holly. Joy." His voice grows urgent. "And if you remember nothing else I've told you, remember this. The deepest joy in life comes from loving someone who loves you, Holly. And no one loves you more than Jesus."

18

Pietro's Pizza Parlor is ablaze with color and sound, a gaudy mixture of Ringling Brothers and country-western. An old-fashioned popcorn machine stands beside several log tables. Popular music blares while video games beep, buzz, and bang. On the opposite wall, silent movies flicker in jerky, jumpy black and white flashes.

Dad looks at the crowd and says, "For a Wednesday night it's awfully busy in here, Holly. You want to eat somewhere else?"

I put the decision back on him. "Whatever you want, Dad."

"You like this place, right? So we'll stay."

What he's saying is that he hates noisy, crowded restaurants, but he'll humor me. I wonder why. In fact, ever since Dad suggested he and I go out for dinner tonight, I've felt puzzled. It has been ages since the two of us have been anywhere by ourselves.

Mom wasn't up to fixing dinner, but that's nothing new. These days Dad usually eats out with a client while I scramble eggs, fry a hamburger, or put in a TV dinner for Mom and me. Why should tonight be different?

It takes twenty minutes for Dad and me to order our pizza, go to the salad bar, and pick up our soft drinks. When we finally maneuver our trays over to a table, Dad looks annoyed. But he winks as he says, "I like it better when a waitress just comes to your table and takes your order."

"This was Neeley's favorite place," I remark. "He'd spend so much time playing video games, his pizza would get cold."

Dad doesn't reply. I feel rebuffed. He still doesn't want us to talk about Neeley.

Dad reaches for the pizza, but I quickly bow my head to thank Jesus silently for the food. I feel self-conscious, but since my talk with Pastor Collins a couple of months ago, I'm determined to make Jesus a bigger part of my life.

Dad bows his head too. Afterward, he says contritely, "We need to get back to saying grace at home."

"I want to," I reply, "but I'm not sure about Mom."

"Well, next time you just go ahead," he tells me. "Mom won't admit it, but I bet she misses it too."

Dad and I help ourselves to hot slices of pepperoni pizza. As we eat, we watch the old-time movie. A bespectacled Harold Lloyd, carrying a ladder, runs out the window of a tall building. Only his ladder catching on the window prevents him from falling. He wiggles and squirms high above the traffic until he maneuvers himself back inside the building. Safety! End of story.

Dad and I watch one reel after another as assorted characters from another era run, jump, and collide hilariously. Keystone cops drive recklessly and narrowly avoid every kind of calamity. We chuckle at the pratfalls of Laurel and Hardy and Buster Keaton.

As Dad spears a tomato wedge from his salad, he muses, "Your Grandfather Rhoades insisted on seeing every Buster Keaton film—not once, but a dozen times!"

"Really? Grandpa Rhoades? You hardly ever mention him."

"Well, he died before you were born, so there's really no reason to talk about him."

"What was he like, Dad?"

Dad's eyes grow reminiscent. "He was a dreamer, Holly. He dabbled in a dozen different things—acting, inventing, woodworking, filmmaking. He dreamed of being another Buster

Keaton, starring in his own films. He was positive he was going to do something to change the world.''

"Did he?''

"No.'' Dad's expression hardens. "He never missed an audition or a casting call, but nothing ever worked out. He couldn't even support his own family. I had to go out and work after high school to help my mother pay the bills.''

"Didn't Grandpa have a real job?''

"That's just it. He had a different job every week. Whatever he could work into his crazy schedule. Some days we'd eat like kings; other days we were lucky to have beans and bread.''

When I don't respond, Dad goes on, "Don't get me wrong, Holly. He was a fascinating man. You and Neeley would have liked Grandpa Rhoades. In fact, Neeley was a lot like him. That's why I pushed Neeley to get a good education and a solid career. I didn't want him becoming a drifter like his grandfather.''

Neeley's name again casts a shadow over our conversation. We both turn our attention back to the funny, frantic actions on the movie screen.

After a while Dad clears his throat and asks, "So are you happy to be out of school for the summer?''

"It's OK.''

"And I guess you're glad to be back at church—''

"I've only been back a couple of Sundays.''

"But it's going well?'' Dad asks.

"I felt funny at first, but everyone treated me nice.''

"I suppose Pastor Collins wonders why your mom and I haven't been back yet.''

"He does ask about you.''

"Well, when your mother's ready, we'll be back in church.''

"When will that be?''

"I wish I knew, Holly.'' Dad finishes his root beer, then looks carefully at me. "I realize things haven't been much fun for you at home lately.''

I look up quizzically.

"I mean,'' he continues, "it'll probably be a while before things get back to normal around the house.''

"Normal?" I echo. "I don't remember what normal is."

Dad's eyes show a hint of disapproval, but he merely traces the ring of his water glass on the table. "You've noticed that your mother's not herself lately," he says with reluctance.

Dad's understatement sends a new ripple of indignation through me. "How could I help but notice? Mom takes so many pills, she's practically a basket case!"

Dad's face twitches slightly. "Don't call her that, Holly."

"But it's true!"

"Mom just can't help herself right now," Dad contends, his voice agitated. "You have no idea how Neeley's death has affected her. It's—it's destroying her."

"It's destroying all of us," I come back stridently.

Dad's eyes narrow. "I would think you could be a little more understanding of your mother."

I feel a swift hurt inside. Staring soberly at Dad, I wonder, *Do you care how Neeley's death has affected me?* But I keep my thoughts to myself and stare down at my pizza. It's cold and unappetizing now. I wish we could just get up and go home.

"Why did we come here?" I mutter.

"You were the one who picked this place, Holly."

"No, I mean, why did we go out to dinner together tonight, Dad?"

In a gesture of frustration, he tosses his napkin onto his plate. "I don't know, Holly. Earlier it seemed like a good idea. I thought if we talked it might help." He gazes despairingly at me. "We have to do something, you know. We have to figure out some way to pick up the pieces and go on, to get beyond these unbearable days."

19

There days after our dinner at the pizza parlor, on a Saturday morning in mid-July, I wake with a start. Strange noises are coming from Neeley's room.

I just out of bed, run into the hall, and nearly collide with Dad. He is carrying a bag crammed with clothes.

"What are you doing?" I ask.

"What I should have done weeks ago, honey. Giving these to the Salvation Army."

"Neeley's clothes?" I exclaim in disbelief.

Dad strides past me toward the stairs. "Someone may as well get some use out of them."

"But they're Neeley's!" I protest.

Unexpectedly, Mom's door opens and she peers at me through glazed, reproachful eyes.

"Mom, do you know what Dad is do—"

"Leave him alone, Holly."

"But he's taking Neeley's things!"

"He's made up his mind, Holly. He says it's for the best."

Dad reappears with a huge cardboard carton. "I need your help, Holly. Will you please sort through Neeley's sketches and pack them in this box?"

"Why? Are you going to give them away too?"

Dad's eyes darken. "No, Holly. I want to store them in the attic."

"But why?" I scream. "Why can't you leave Neeley's room alone? Why do you have to change it?"

"Don't you understand, Holly? We talked about it at dinner the other night. We have to put things behind us and get on with our lives."

"But this is Neeley's room!"

"It's not Neeley's room anymore. From now on it'll have to be the—the guest room."

"Guest room?" I scoff. "We don't have guests. No one comes here anymore!"

Dad hands me the box and says, "Let's not waste time, Holly. Get dressed and get busy. If you find some things of Neeley's you'd like as keepsakes, that's fine. But I'd like to clear everything out of here today if I can."

I watch in silent fury as Dad empties another of Neeley's dresser drawers onto the bed. I look pleadingly at Mom in the doorway. "Please don't let him!"

Oblivious of me, Mom pulls her summer robe tighter around her. Then, with slow, mechanical motions she shuffles back into her room and shuts the door behind her.

I stare tearfully at the closed door. So! I have no choice but to help Dad remove the last vestiges of Neeley from our lives. Back in my own room, I pull on my Levi's and one of Neeley's old T-shirts. Then grudgingly I kick the cardboard carton along the floor into Neeley's bedroom and begin the painful task of sorting his drawings.

Minutes later, I come across a disturbing sketch in blacks and grays of a man standing alone on a precipice. The man looks like Neeley. Scrawled beneath the sketch in Neeley's handwriting is a poem:

> Too many spaces between people.
> Blanks!
> Where are the bridges?
> How do I cross over?
> I might as well be on
> The dark side of the moon.

Fresh tears well in my eyes. I never realized until now how alone Neeley must have felt. Didn't he know I was here for him? Or didn't it matter?

I blink and turn quickly to several watercolor sketches. One is a portrait of me in my pink graduation dress from junior high. Neeley painted it last spring. He made me prettier than I am, but he said that was how I looked to him. In jest he had scribbled under it, "Someday when I'm famous, this will be worth a million dollars—your big brother, Neeley."

Tears spring unbidden again. I crush the sketch against my chest and run to my own room. I place the portrait in my bottom dresser drawer with my photo albums, scrap books, and teen magazines. Then I throw myself on my bed and muffle my sobs in my pillow.

After a while I roll over on my back and stare at the ceiling. I concentrate on my heart pounding under my ribs, steady, constant. Glubity-glub. Over and over.

What is it like when your heart stops beating?

I find myself thinking gruesome thoughts about Neeley—about the night I found him in his room motionless and dying, about how his heart isn't beating anymore, and about how his body is buried in the ground. My skin turns clammy at the nightmare images. I feel as if Neeley has died all over again today, not almost three months ago.

That's something I am learning. When someone you love dies, it isn't just a one-time death you have to get used to. It's a thousand little deaths of everyday things that were part of Neeley. These little deaths are like sudden slaps that catch me unaware. They rub the pain raw again, like broken scabs.

I force my mind onto a more pleasant track: Lori and her father and their patient, loving concern. Two months ago, I thought Pastor Collins' words would work magic and immediately make everything right again. I figured if I prayed and read my Bible every day, my hurt over Neeley would go away.

But not that much has changed. Mom and Dad are still the same. I'm the same. Except I know now there's a way through the darkness. Jesus is the way. That's a fact. I know it in my head. Now I have to learn it in my heart.

I've been trying to do the things Pastor Collins suggested. He said I should read my Bible and pray every day, even if I don't feel like it. He told me to write out Scripture verses and tape them to my dresser mirror. Now my mirror is dotted with slips of paper that say, "God is love," "To live is Christ," "Perfect love casts out fear," and "We love because he first loved us."

I'm also writing down my feelings in a diary. Pastor Collins said it might help me to work out my grief. I'm not sure what he means by "work out." He makes it sound like hard labor, like working at a job or doing chores. Maybe that's how it is. It feels that way.

When I pray I try to think of Jesus instead of myself. But it isn't easy. Even now, this very minute, when I pray I catch myself turning back to my own hurts. I begin: *Dear Jesus, I love you. Help me to be more loving and kind to Mom and Dad.*

But how can I be when Dad's acting so unreasonable today? And Mom takes so many pills. They don't care about my feelings. But what do I care? I don't need them anyway!

Oh, Jesus, I'm doing it again. I'm sorry. I want to think about You, not me. I want to remember how much You love me, not worry whether Mom or Dad care.

But they don't act like they care. Why can't they be like other parents? Do I have to die like Neeley before they realize they love me too?

Oh, no! Me again? Oh, Jesus, help me to forget myself. Help me to think about You. I love You. I do. But the hurt won't go away. Please make it better. Jesus, please rock me to sleep in Your arms so I'll forget.

Lying here on my bed, I think again about all the things Pastor Collins told me. I know what he said is true. But knowing something doesn't make it happen. I wanted God to change everything at once. I wanted Him to make Mom and Dad and me happy again.

Pastor Collins told me I shouldn't depend on my feelings. They change. He said I should rest on the promises of God in His Word. I'm trying.

In his sermon last Sunday, Pastor Collins explained that God doesn't exist to make us happy. *We* exist to worship Him. I hope someday I can love God without *me* always getting in the way.

Lori told me after church that her dad is hoping my folks will go see a mental health counselor. Those are fancy words for a shrink. Maybe he thinks my parents are crazy because they won't go back to church. He told Lori he hoped we would seek counseling together as a family.

How can he think Mom and Dad would talk about Neeley to a stranger when they hardly even talk about him to me?

Suddenly I hear Dad's voice calling outside my door. "Holly, come on! You've still got work to do."

I scramble off my bed and dash back to Neeley's room. I find Dad removing the art prints from the walls. He works methodically, stripping the room of all that once was Neeley. Resentment flares inside me. I want to scream, *You won, Dad! You never understood Neeley's art! Now you can get rid of it forever!*

But an unspoken accusations vanish when Dad turns my way. I spot tiny rivulets of tears tracing the creases around his eyes. He pivots before I look too closely. I glance elsewhere, embarrassed to have glimpsed Dad's pain.

We work for hours, packing away Neeley's things, speaking only when necessary. Mom appears briefly from time to time to survey our progress. She watches us with a sad, flat expression, then retreats wordlessly back to her room.

The last thing to go is Neeley's sculpture. In a melancholy voice, Dad says, "I'll need some help carrying this to the attic, Holly."

"Not the attic," I protest. "Can't it stay here?"

We argue. We compromise. The clay bust will be stored in Neeley's closet out of sight. Another small ritual to whitewash Neeley from our lives.

Around five, the doorbell rings. I trudge downstairs pushing back damp strands of hair from my forehead. I open the door to a gangly blond young man with pale gray eyes. I give him my perturbed *Whatcha sellin'?* look.

"I'm here about the car," he says politely.

"Car?"

"Yes. The Chevy. You haven't sold it yet, have you?"

"There must be some mistake."

The boy waves a newspaper in my face. "It says right here you have a restored '56 Chevy in mint condition. Reasonably priced."

My mouth drops open in surprise. "You mean—Neeley's car?"

The boy looks flustered. "Is it available or not? I'd like to look it over."

Outrage paralyzes me. The youth interprets my silence as consent. "If the price is right," he rushes on, "I'll bring my dad over tonight to check it out."

Finding my voice, I reply in a shout of anger, "The car's not for sale! It belongs to my brother, Neeley! It's his, do you understand? No one else can have it!"

"Holly!"

I whirl around in the doorway to face my father. "Go back inside," he tells me, his gaze piercing. Then he turns to the bewildered youth and says placatingly, "I'm sorry for the misunderstanding. You're here about the ad? Well, the car's in the garage. Come with me."

I start to follow them, but Mom's voice stops me. "Why were you shouting, Holly?" she asks accusingly from the stairs.

"Dad's going to sell Neeley's car!"

Mom looks away.

"You knew about this, didn't you?"

She pauses, then says in a detached tone, "Yes. It was your father's decision."

"But Neeley loved that car!"

"I don't want to talk about it, Holly."

"You don't want to talk about anything anymore!" I retort.

Mom starts back upstairs. I run after her. "Please, let me have the car, Mom!"

She glances back, irritation coloring her voice. "You're too young to drive, Holly."

"I'll be fifteen pretty soon," I argue. "When I'm sixteen I can get my driver's license."

"A car can't sit idle for over a year waiting for someone to drive it."

I grip Mom's arm entreatingly. "Please don't let Dad sell Neeley's car!"

Mom stiffens. "I wish I could help, Holly, but I can't. I've got to go upstairs. I have a splitting headache."

I release her and, in desperation, run outside after Dad. He's just coming up the porch steps. "Looks like we may have a buyer," he says matter-of-factly while I catch my breath. "The boy and I are taking her out for a spin. If he likes the car, I think he'll be back tonight with his father and a check."

"You can't do it," I pant.

"I'm sorry, honey. It's done."

20

Just before dark I slip outside to the driveway where Neeley's blue Chevy sits waiting for its new owner. On impulse I climb into the driver's seat. I lean back and summon memories of Neeley sitting here, talking casually as he drives. I imagine that I'm Neeley. I am Neeley Rhoades, sitting here enjoying my car on a plain, ordinary day. Gently I run my hands over the steering wheel, savoring the feel of worn leather. The scent of Neeley's after-shave still lingers in the air—or is it only my imagination? Marsha's scarf hangs from the rearview mirror, faded now, an ironic reminder of Neeley's spurned devotion. Surprisingly, the key is in the ignition, where that pimply-faced blond boy—the boy who wants to buy Neeley's car—left it after his test drive.

I can't tolerate the idea of Neeley's car belonging to a stranger. Irrationally, I wonder, *What if Neeley comes back and his car is gone!*

Another voice inside me answers, *He's never coming back*, but I shut it out. I don't want to hear it. I feel an intense loyalty to Neeley. Haven't I always been the only one who understood him? The only one who really appreciated him? *He had to die before Mom and Dad realized how much they loved him.*

I'm not sure why I do it, but I turn on the ignition. I listen to the motor purring. "Still sounds pretty good, doesn't it, Neeley?" I say aloud. The sound of the engine spurs a sensation of energy inside me, a sense of daring.

I could drive this car if I wanted to!

"You let me drive once, Neeley," I say, my courage growing. "You showed me how. You cheered me on. You made me feel as if I could do anything, go anywhere. I wanted to drive forever."

An idea comes to me: *If I take your car, Neeley, no one else can have it.*

I shift the automobile into reverse. It jerks and groans momentarily until the gear finds its proper niche. Gingerly I press my foot on the gas pedal. *I'm moving.* Down the driveway. Over the curb. I'm in the street now. Shift into low. Careful, don't grind the gears. OK, give it some gas. Hey, I'm on my way. Down the street, past all the familiar houses.

No one is watching. That's good. Then they can't try to stop me. I'm approaching an intersection. Don't panic. Who has the right of way? I do. The cross street has a stop sign.

I drive Neeley's route through the residential section toward town. But the traffic is heavier than I expected. It's dusk. The sun is a huge red ball on the horizon. Its rays glare on the windshield, making me squint. I sit forward. My muscles feel tense, almost rigid.

I pass familiar landmarks. The Sears store, a McDonald's with its golden arches, the art supplies store.

The car behind me honks. I glance down at the speedometer. Twenty miles . . . in a thirty-five mile zone. I accelerate timidly. My palms are moist. The driver honks again, closing in, tailgating, practically climbing my bumper!

Flustered, I press my foot on the gas. The car spurts ahead. Gripping the wheel, I push my foot almost to the floor. I feel out of control, terrified. I nearly clip several parked cars and narrowly miss one approaching auto after another. The world rushes at me crazily, streets converge, lights flash, and vehicles appear out of nowhere. I'm dizzy, light-headed.

A thought startles me: *I could crash. I could die.* Then another idea: *I want to die. I want to be with Neeley.*

I head out of town toward the freeway. I'm not sure how much time has passed. I know only that night has curtained the world with Neeley's favorite color, ultramarine blue. I fumble with several knobs, trying to locate the headlights.

"You should be here, Neeley," I assert. "I need you. I drove better when you were with me. I did everything better."

Unexpectedly I begin to cry. "Neeley, I won't ever forget you!" I wail. "Help me to understand, that's all I ask. Just this one thing—why, Neeley? Didn't you know how we'd feel? Didn't you care? You just left like it was nothing at all, and you never even said goodbye!"

My sobs mix with spasms of hiccups. I'm trembling so badly I can hardly drive. A dozen different emotions clash within me, short-circuiting one another. "Are you listening to me, Neeley?" I plead. "I feel so helpless and confused. I want to be your little sister again. I love you so much, Neeley!"

But only the wind answers as it whistles bleakly through the cogs and crevices of Neeley's car: *Neeley isn't here. He'll never reply.*

"I hate you, Neeley Rhoades!" I utter back in fury. "How could you just go away and leave me behind? Oh God, when will the hurting stop!"

I spot a freeway offramp ahead. A huge red sign with phosphorescent letters warns Do Not Enter.

I'm going to anyway. I swerve Neeley's Chevy sharply to the right and head the wrong way up the offramp. Pavement reflectors shine red in my headlights. Suddenly, great, glaring globes of light fill my windshield. An automobile bears down on me, its horn blasting through the chill night air.

In a fraction of a second I see myself dead and in heaven with Neeley. Instantly I realize I don't want to die.

Before I can even scream to God for help, the approaching vehicle veers around me, its tires screeching. I swerve onto the shoulder, out of-control, flying over gravel. My car careens toward an embankment. I fly forward into an explosion of fireworks and chaos. As metal collides with concrete, my world dissolves in darkness.

21

Even with my eyes closed I'm aware of bright lights above me. And peculiar sounds—distant, muted whispers, and metallic noises. Someone nearby is repeating my name. *Holly.* Over and over. Urgently.

Am I in heaven? I can't be. My head hurts too much.

It's Mom's voice. She's beside me. I struggle to open my eyes. My lids feel as if a giant is pressing them down. The giant must be sitting on my forehead. I want to shake him off, but it takes all my effort to force my eyelids open. They barely flutter.

I hear another voice. A man's. But not my dad. A stranger. I attempt to focus on what he is saying, but the words won't quite hang together. "A close call, Mr. and Mrs. Rhoades. Wait and see . . . when she regains consciousness."

Dad's voice now. "But she will be all right, won't she?"

"Physically, yes. But emotionally—"

"You—you think she was trying to kill herself, don't you?"

A long pause. "The possibility can't be ruled out, Mr. Rhoades."

"How could she," cries Mom, "after Neeley?"

The doctor speaks again. "Your husband told me about your son, Mrs. Rhoades. I'm sorry. But often, when a person commits suicide, there's a tendency for others in his circle of acquaintances to consider it too. Perhaps that's what happened with your daughter."

Mom's voice breaks as she murmurs, "Oh, God, no! I can't cope with another one. I just can't!"

Dad asks, "What can we do, doctor? We both feel so helpless."

Another pause. I try again to open my eyes. My lids flicker slightly. The light is excruciating.

The doctor clears his throat and says, "Perhaps the accident was a cry for help. Talk to your daughter about it, Mr. Rhoades. Be open, honest. Confront her with your suspicions."

"You mean tell her we think she tried to kill herself? Wouldn't that just be putting ideas into her head?"

"Not really. Most parents will do anything to avoid confrontations with their children. But suicidal youngsters often feel unloved, out of control. They need someone to take charge and show them they're loved. Draw your daughter into conversation. Find out where she's hurting. Let her know you're there for her. Talk *with* her, not *at* her."

"You seem to have the answers sewn up in a neat little package," remarks Dad bitterly.

The doctor makes a sound, not quite a cough. "Well, Mr. Rhoades, I've seen enough cases like this to know that simple communication between parents and children is the key to preventing suicide." There is silence. The doctor continues. "What I'm saying is that the most common factor among young suicide victims is the absence of strong parental relationships."

"I tried talking to her just a couple of days ago," says Dad defensively. "She gave no indication she was this upset."

"Genuine communication isn't something that happens in a day or even weeks, Mr. Rhoades. It takes time and patience on both sides. But without it—"

"What you're saying is that our son's death—it *was* our fault," says Mom unevenly.

"It was not," snaps Dad.

"I always knew it," continues Mom shrilly. "I've felt so guilty!"

"Guilt doesn't do anyone any good, Mrs. Rhoades," the doctor stresses. "Your family will be better off if you concentrate on the good things you still have."

"Good things?" challenges Dad.

"Yes, Mr. Rhoades. You still have one another."

I make an effort to lift my bandaged head, but the pain is too severe.

"Look, she's moving," exclaims Mom.

I feel my parents hovering over me. Someone takes my hand and rubs it. The doctor calls my name. This time I manage to open my eyes.

"How do you feel, Holly?" the doctor asks.

I moan.

"You're in the hospital, honey," Dad says shakily. "You had an accident, but you're going to be OK."

"What . . . happened?"

"Your head hit the windshield, Holly, and your ribs were bruised by the steering wheel," explains the physician. "You'll be sore for a few days."

"Oh, Holly!" Mom leans over and kisses me. Her cheek is wet. Her touch reminds me of nights from my childhood when she rocked me to sleep in her arms, when I was safe, cuddled, cherished.

Dad bends over and kisses me too. "How's my girl?" he says anxiously, his eyes searching mine. I wonder, *When did wrinkles start marring his rugged face?*

I try to swallow. My mouth feels crusty dry. It's hard to speak. "I'm sorry . . . about Neeley's car—"

"It doesn't matter, Holly," says Dad, "as long as you're all right."

"She'll be fine," the doctor assures us. "We're going to keep her under observation for a day or two and run some tests. Routine stuff. You should get some sleep now, Holly, and visit with your folks in the morning."

Mom and Dad seem reluctant to leave. They linger by my bedside. I fall asleep comforted by their concern.

After breakfast the next morning, Mom and Dad return. I'm sitting up in bed, awake. My head still hurts. "Can I go home now?" I beg.

"Let's wait and see what the doctor says," replies Dad.

"I don't like it here."

Mom looks worried. "Why not?"

I glare at my liquid breakfast—tasteless bouillon, lukewarm tea, and melting Jell-O. "If I have to eat hospital food, I'll really be sick." I don't add that I hate being in this dismal place where Neeley died. Everything about it—the gray walls, bustling nurses, and creaking gurneys—reminds me of the night we brought Neeley in.

"How do you feel?" asks Mom, sitting in the chair by my bed.

"Lousy."

"Well, when you feel better, Lori and Richard will be by to see you."

"Richard? Oh, Mom, I can't let him see me like this!"

"You look a hundred percent better than you did last night."

"I look like a genie from the magic lamp with this weird turban on my head."

Mom takes my hand. "The bandages will come off in a day or so."

"Did you sleep well?" Dad questions. He looks uneasy as he paces absently between my bed and the window.

"They wouldn't let me sleep," I reply peevishly. "First, a nurse woke me up to give me a pill. Then she took my blood pressure and stuck a thermometer in my mouth. Then early this morning someone in the next room was playing elevator music."

"Elevator music?" repeats Dad.

Mom smiles at Dad. "*Our* kind of music, dear."

Dad chuckles half-heartedly. He seems to have something else on his mind. After a minute he approaches my bed and gazes at me. His eyes are troubled. "Holly," he begins, his shoulders tensing, "the doctor suggested we talk to you about the—the accident."

"Not yet, Stewart," Mom cuts in.

"We can't put this off, Marge," argues Dad.

I look questioningly at Dad, then at Mom.

"What your father means, Holly," Mom says hesitantly, "is that we want to be sure it *was* an accident."

"What do you mean?" I ask warily.

Dad's voice grows a bit gruff. "Holly, you must admit it was a foolhardy thing to take Neeley's car."

"But I didn't plan to take it."

Mom draws close. "But the way you drove onto that freeway offramp—" Her voice rises precariously. "You didn't do it on purpose, did you, Holly?"

I look blankly at them. Then it sinks in. "You think I tried to—kill myself?"

"Did you, Holly?" Dad asks urgently.

I start to say no, then I pause. "I don't know."

"You mean you did consider it?" persists Dad.

Suddenly I feel flustered, defensive. "I don't know, Daddy. I don't know what I was trying to do!"

Mom is practically in tears. "How could you even think of it, Holly, after all we've been through?"

A bolt of anger charges through me. I want to shout, *What about what I've been through!* Instead, I say defiantly, "It's my life, and I'll do what I want with it!"

Mom is weeping now. I wish I could bite my tongue, but my pride won't let me retract my words.

Mom wipes her eyes with her handkerchief. Then she straightens her shoulders and stares at me with an expression I've never seen before. Her voice swells with conviction. "I never had a chance to say this to Neeley, Holly, but I've thought about it many times, and now I'm saying it to you. It is *not* your life. God gave it to you, and only He should be able to take it away."

I gaze at my hands, ashamed. I know Pastor Collins would tell me the same thing, but I'm not about to admit it to Mom.

Mom isn't finished. "If you kill yourself, Holly, you're stealing parts of all of us—your family and friends, even your teachers. We've all invested pieces of ourselves in you. We've got a stake in what happens to you." She pauses, trembling, and draws in a breath. "If you kill yourself, you kill us too!"

Now I'm crying. Not just from shame. Something more. "Isn't that what you and Dad are doing too?" I counter bitterly. "Mom, you take pills until you can't see straight, and Dad is working himself to death. How can you tell me how to live?"

Mom looks stricken. She sinks back slightly. "Oh, Holly. Is that how we seem to you?"

My sobs break in a torrent of anguish. "You don't even care whether we're a family. Neeley's the only one you think about anymore!"

Mom takes me in her arms. "Oh, Holly, we still want to be a family. We've just forgotten how."

Dad hovers nearby, looking embarrassed. Then he squeezes in for a hug too. "I love you, baby," he whispers, his voice rough with emotion.

My arms circle his neck. "I love you too, Daddy. I don't want to hide my feelings from you like Neeley did. I want us to be a real family."

Dad murmurs against my ear, "With God's help, we will be, honey."

22

Richard and I are sitting together in a booth at McDonald's. He's eating a Big Mac. I ordered a Happy Meal. I feel like being a kid again. I sit munching my cheeseburger and watching the children play in the kiddieland outside. There are slides and swings and teeter-totters painted bright red, blue, green, and yellow. I wish I were little enough to play on them again.

I watch a boy and girl climb the slide. They must be brother and sister; they're both wearing Mickey Mouse T-shirts and crisp new Levi's. He's older, maybe nine, maybe too old for the slide, too old to squeal with delight like the girl is doing. She can't be more than five.

I watch her glide down the gleaming, spiraling chute, her arms high, her mouth open in a great, echoing shriek. Her brother follows close behind, but he sits rigid and his expression is contained, as if he wants people to think he'd rather be doing something else.

They go down the slide again and again, their expressions always the same. She screams; he looks bored. Sometimes they run to a woman standing nearby, obviously their mother. She is holding a soft drink and french fries. Sometimes she pops a fry into the girl's mouth, as if they were baby bird and mommy bird; sometimes she holds out the soft drink to the boy, and he sips thirstily.

They could be Neeley and me ten years ago, I muse silently. Older brother, younger sister. Neeley was as cautious with his fun as this boy and just as concerned that he not be considered silly or childish. And I—I was as oblivious of the world and caught up in myself as this little laughing girl.

She'll learn, I muse solemnly. *She'll realize it's not all fun and games. But will she learn before it's too late?*

"You look awfully serious, Holly," says Richard crushing his hamburger wrapper in a little ball and pitching it at me.

I catch it without thinking and pitch it back. "I was just watching the kids outside."

"Nothing better to do, huh?"

"I'm sorry, Richard. Do you feel slighted?"

"Naw. I'm used to being ignored. I'm just that sorta guy."

I laugh. "No, you're not. I'm not ignoring you. Not intentionally. I just—" How can I explain to Richard the hard time I have concentrating on things lately, the way my mind wanders without warning? Maybe it has something to do with my head injury, or maybe it's just another after-effect of Neeley's death.

"You don't have to explain, Holly. It's OK. I was just giving you a hard time. In fact, my conscience is already bugging me. I should be nice to a girl who just got out of the hospital."

I look away. "I don't want to be reminded of that place, OK?"

Richard looks chagrined. "I guess I'm batting zero today, huh?"

"No, you're not. You bought me a Happy Meal, didn't you? And now I have my very own Goofy Go-cart for a prize. What more could I want?"

He smiles invitingly. "A chocolate shake? A walk home in the moonlight? A steady guy for the summer?"

I stare at him in amazement. "Are you serious? A shake, a walk, a steady guy? Like, is there some kind of message here?"

He sips his Coke, pretending not to hear me.

"Come on, Richard. You can't just say something like that and let it drop."

He grins at me. "So, OK, we'll start with the shake."

I lean forward, my elbows on the table. "Listen, Richard, you know you're my best friend, after Lori."

"OK. 'Best friends' isn't bad. For starts." He gives me that certain look, his eyes crinkling in a way that makes my stomach turn somersaults. I feel my face flushing with warmth.

"Why are you looking at me that way, Richard?"

"I don't know. Maybe because I almost lost you. It scared me, Holly. *You* scared me."

"I scared myself, Richard. I can't believe I'd do something so stupid as drive my brother's car."

"Yeah, driving when you don't know how does top your 'Stupidest Things to Do' list. Tops mine too."

"But I learned a lesson, Richard." I touch the bandage on my forehead. "This scar will always remind me how foolish I was."

Richard helps himself to my french fries. "So are things any better now at home?"

I shrug. "It's too soon to tell. It's like we're all walking around on pins and needles. No one wants to upset anyone else. Mom and Dad are scared I'll go off the deep end again. I'm afraid Mom will go back on her pills. Dad's trying to stay home more, but he's as jumpy as a cat on a hot stove. I don't know, Richard. Do you think we'll ever be normal again?"

He reaches for my hand and holds it protectively. "You will be, Holly. Take my word for it."

"I'll try." I love it when Richard is so masterful and take-charge, although I'd never tell him that. Somehow, with Richard, I feel special—and safe. It's different between us than it was last year or even a few months ago. Better. I can't even put it into words, but it's like we're both becoming different people . . . but growing *together*.

"You ready for that walk home now?" he asks. "It's a little early for the moonlight, but if we walk slowly enough, who knows?"

I reach for my purse and tuck in my Goofy Go-cart, my silly little souvenir of today. But just as I'm about to slip out of the booth, I hear a girl's voice chanting, "Holly? Holly Rhoades, is that you?"

I look up just as Melba Harris, a gangly, gaudy girl from my algebra class, rushes over and flings her arms around me like a long-lost cousin. "Holly, how are you?" she exclaims in her grating, sing-song voice. Melba is one of those bubble-brained types I usually try to avoid, but there's no evading her today.

"Oh, Holly, I read about your accident, and I thought it was the most dreadful thing I ever heard of—the absolute pits! What terrible luck your family has had—especially after your brother died so recently! Your parents must be beside themselves. Are you OK? You could have been killed, you know. Whatever possessed you to drive your brother's car like that? You must have been out of your mind with grief. Oh, look at that nasty bandage. You poor thing!"

I pull back, disengaging myself from Melba's grip. "I'm fine, Melba. Really."

"We were just leaving," Richard interjects, steering me away from Melba Motor-mouth.

"Oh, well, I guess you wouldn't be here at McDonald's if you weren't OK." Her voice trails off. "I'll tell everyone I see that you're doing fine in spite of everything . . ."

"You do that, Melba," says Richard dryly as we dart out the door.

All the way home Richard and I laugh over Melba the Meddlesome Magpie (Richard's name for her). Actually, I feel enraged over her remarks, her false solicitation, her intrusiveness and insensitivity. "I should have thrown a milkshake in her face, or tripped her, or stuffed a Big Mac down her throat," I complain.

"Come on, you're too nice to do any of those things," Richard chides as we fall into step together.

"Yeah, but I can imagine doing them, and that feels almost as good as the real thing."

Richard slips his arm around me as we walk. "Aw, the Melbas of this world don't mean any harm, Holly. They've got their problems too. They're their own worst enemy. Can you imagine what it's going to be like when the Motor-mouth tries to find a job someday—or a husband?"

"He'd better be deaf." I giggle in spite of myself.

"If he's not, he soon will be," Richard quips. "She'd drive him absolutely bonkers."

We both break into hysterics as Richard mimics Melba. I laugh until my sides hurt. Somehow Richard has made my whole encounter with Melba seem hilarious. It feels wonderful to laugh at something that days ago would have made me cry. Instinctively I know that if I can laugh now at Melba's antics, then yes, truly, I am surviving.

When we reach my front door, to my total amazement Richard bends down and brushes my lips with a kiss . . . and suddenly, being alive takes on a whole new meaning.

23

Lori and I walk barefoot along a deserted stretch of beach.
The sand is prickly hot. The late August sun glistens on the water
like rainbows rippling over glass. Seagulls swoop above us,
screeching hungrily.

Mom and Dad are relaxing over in the picnic area, where
Dad barbecued hamburgers for lunch. It has been six weeks
since my accident. This is our first real outing together since
Neeley died. We're working at being an ordinary family again.
But I'm glad Lori came with us today. Somehow she makes it
easier to have fun.

"Your parents look good," she remarks as we approach the
water and burrow our toes into the cool, wet sand.

"Mom's trying not to take any more pills," I respond.
"And Dad is working fewer hours. We've been eating some
meals together again, so Mom has a reason to cook."

"How are your headaches?"

"I rarely have them anymore."

"I'm glad," replies Lori. "The scar on your forehead hardly shows now."

"How can you tell?" I laugh. "You left your glasses in
your purse."

"I noticed *before*."

"Oh well, makeup works wonders," I answer wryly.

"I'm glad your parents have come back to church," Lori
continues, squinting against the bright sunlight.

"They were surprised by how friendly and kind everyone was." Looking thoughtfully at Lori, I add, "I just wish it hadn't taken my accident . . . smashing up Neeley's car—"

"Does it still bother you?"

"I think about it sometimes. I remember what the police said when they were preparing their accident report. They said I could have killed someone, Lori. Not just myself, but innocent people. They said I needed to realize the—the enormity of my actions."

"Do you?"

"Now I do. I don't even know who I was the night I took Neeley's car. It was like someone else inside me. But I've asked God to forgive me. And Dad says I have to put off getting my driver's license an extra year." I sigh in resignation. "I'm just thankful the accident wasn't worse."

Lori smiles. "Me too. I don't ever want to lose my best friend."

I smile back. "You know, having Bible study with you these past few weeks has really helped."

"It's been special praying together too," Lori agrees. She leans down and picks up a broken shell and examines it.

"God is answering our prayers," I note. "Things are going lots better at my house."

"That's great!" says Lori as she hands me the shell.

I turn it over in my hand. The inside is pearly pink. "Did you know your father arranged for my mom and dad and me to meet with a Christian counselor?"

"Yes. When did you go?"

"We had our second meeting last Tuesday night." I rub the moist sand from the shell and hand it back to Lori.

"Were you scared?" she asks.

I hesitate, then confess, "Yeah. So were Mom and Dad."

"But you went anyway?"

I nod. "Your dad said counseling will help us learn to share our feelings with each other."

For a long time Lori and I walk along the water, absorbed in conversation. This is a rare treat for us. Usually, at home or at church or school, we're surrounded by other people. I feel almost as if I am back in the carefree days of other summers when my main concern was little more than getting an even tan or a new bicycle for trips to the beach.

Lori and I stop chatting when we spot a group of teenagers playing volleyball on the beach. We pause to watch one tall, muscular boy spike the ball over the net. Then Lori nudges me. "Are my nearsighted eyes deceiving me, or is that Marsha Piper?"

My gaze follows Lori's to a striking brunette with a golden tan, poised to hit the ball. "Oh, no," I gasp. "Let's get out of here."

Lori grips my elbow. "Why? Aren't you even going to say hello?"

How can I possibly explain to Lori the sinking sensation I feel or the painful memories of Neeley that Marsha stirs inside me? Pulling away, I snap, "Come on, before she sees us."

Then I remember my last encounter with Marsha—at Neeley's funeral. I recall the hurt in her eyes when she asked if Neeley's death was her fault. *What do you think?* I had slammed back, gladly heaping the guilt on her shoulders. I wanted her to feel as bad as I felt. But I was wrong.

I glance back tentatively at Marsha. For an instant our eyes meet, then she looks away as if she doesn't recognize me.

OK, if that's how she wants it, I decide. *I did my part*. But somehow I can't make myself walk away. I look again in Marsha's direction. She fumbles the ball twice in a row. Then she signals to another girl and says, "I need a break. Take my place, OK?"

Marsha strolls toward me in her usual confident manner. She's wearing the most gorgeous bathing suit I've ever seen.

"Hi, Holly, I thought that was you," she says, offering her coolly appraising smile.

"Hi, Marsha," I mumble self-consciously. Somehow I feel stark naked even though my swimsuit covers lots more than Marsha's does. "This is Lori Collins," I introduce. "Lori, Marsha Piper."

"Hi, Lori. Say, didn't I meet you at . . . " Marsha's voice trails off. Her composed expression falters.

"At Neeley's funeral?" Lori supplies. "I'm Pastor Collins's daughter."

"Yes, I remember now." Marsha glances back at the volleyball game. "Well, I guess I'd better get back—"

I can't let Marsha go yet. There's something I need to say. "Marsha, I was just wondering—" I begin.

She gazes curiously at me.

"The last time we talked I said something."

Marsha's eyes darken. Her mouth settles into a pout.

"I said it was your fault."

Marsha's eyes blaze defiantly. "I don't have to listen to this, you know."

"No, I didn't mean that," I rush on nervously. "I just want you to know Neeley's death *wasn't* your fault."

Marsha's eyes widen. "Not my fault? But you said—"

"I was hurt and angry," I explain. "I wanted to blame someone. So I blamed you."

Marsha looks down and seems absorbed in digging a hole in the sand with her toe. "It was a logical choice," she concedes. "I broke up with Neeley. I lied to him. I hurt him terribly."

I stare at Marsha in astonishment. "You—you really do blame yourself, don't you?"

"Why not? It's true." She gives a fatalistic shrug. "I have to live with it."

"No, Marsha," I persist. "That's what I'm trying to tell you. You don't have to feel guilty about Neeley."

Marsha studies me suspiciously. "I don't know what this is all about."

"I feel guilty about Neeley too, Marsha," I continue earnestly, "but Jesus took away the guilt. I know Jesus loves me . . . and He loves you too."

Marsha emits a hollow little laugh. "Is this a sermon or what?"

"No. I just don't want you to feel guilty anymore about Neeley."

"What do you care? You must hate me."

I look blankly at Marsha. "Hate you? No. I guess I did at first, but now I—I just want you to know that Jesus cares and wants to help you."

Marsha brushes away a reluctant tear trickling down her cheek. "Maybe we can talk again sometime," she says. She pivots and starts back toward her friends. "I gotta get back to the game, Holly. We—we'll be in touch, OK?"

Lori and I wave politely, turn, and head back up the beach toward the picnic area. "Holly, you were terrific," Lori gushes.

I laugh lightly. "You must be kidding. I'm not sure she even listened to me."

"But you tried. You had the courage to talk to her."

I look over at Lori. "It's funny." I sigh. "I still don't like Marsha. But I could feel God's love for her inside me. It was weird . . . and neat, at the same time."

"Like my dad would say, you did the loving, considerate thing," muses Lori. "Neeley would be proud of you."

The idea of Neeley being proud of me unexpectedly chokes me up. I look away and call brightly, "Race you into the water, Lori!"

"Not fair!" she cries. "You're twenty pounds lighter!" We scramble along the beach, kicking up sand, and wade into the cold water up to our waists. We swim for a while; then, breathless and shivering, we lie back on the water and float, closing our eyes against the dazzling sun.

Eventually Lori glances my way and says, "Isn't this relaxing, Holly? Makes you feel as if all's right with the world."

All is right with *me*, I realize with surprise. As I relax my muscles and allow the waves to carry me, an insight takes shape in my mind. Being kind to Marsha just now was a choice for Jesus. And my love for Him grows as I choose Him again and again in a dozen small ways every day.

Choices. So many choices. The choice to think about the Lord Jesus instead of my own pain, to sing a song instead of complaining, to call Lori or Richard for encouragement instead of sulking in my room, to pray for Mom and Dad instead of criticizing them. The choices are mine to make. I don't have to feel helpless anymore.

I look over at Lori a few feet away and tell her, "I could float like this forever, couldn't you?"

"Fer sure." She laughs.

We float a while longer. Then we turn over and tread water side by side, reminiscing.

"Remember last summer when Neeley taught us to swim?" says Lori.

"How could I forget? Richard even videotaped us, remember?"

"Do I! I nearly died of embarrassment. I was crazy about Neeley even then," Lori recalls.

"Yeah. You must have pretended you were drowning a dozen times so he would rescue you."

"Well, if I remember right, Neeley had a terrible time teaching you to float on your back."

I laugh, remembering, and nearly swallow a mouthful of water. For Lori's benefit I imitate Neeley's strong tenor voice. "He would insist, 'You've got to trust yourself to the water, Holly. Believe you'll float, and you will.' But invariably I sank."

"For an older brother, he showed amazing patience," remarks Lori.

"He was the greatest," I reflect solemnly.

For several minutes I float again on my back. I concentrate on the water buoying me along gently with its steady, surging rhythm. I recall my many tries and failures before I summoned the courage to simply lie back and let the water do the work. What a glorious sense of freedom I felt once I let myself go to the water.

Trusting Christ is like that, I realize suddenly. If only Neeley could have let go and relaxed and let God carry him along in His love. Then God would have been enough for Neeley.

But I can't keep thinking about what might have been. I roll over and swim toward Lori. "Want to go in?" I sputter through the froth.

"It's up to you," she gasps as she paddles over beside me.

"Mom brought a huge watermelon. Are you hungry?"

"Of course! This just happens to be the week of my watermelon diet!"

"You got it!" I chuckle. *Neeley's favorite expression.*

Minutes later Lori and I trudge with sopping hair and gritty, sunburned skin to the picnic area. My sinuses ache, and my reddening shoulders sting. We take turns making cutting jokes about ourselves.

Me: "We smell like rotting seaweed."

Lori: "And dead fish!"

Me: "We look like drowned rats."

Lori: "One scrawny, one roly-poly."

I push back my bedraggled mop and snicker. "No rat ever had to worry about chipped nails and chapped lips."

"Not to mention runny mascara," Lori banters. She squints mockingly. "If I leave my glasses off, I won't have to look at us."

"OK. I'll wear your goggles—er, glasses, and be blind too!"

We laugh, breathless and exhausted, deliriously exuberant for a few fleeting moments under the lush summer sun. Almost I forget about Neeley. But not quite. He will always be there—in every face, in every voice, in all my memories. I guess the hurt will never go away completely. But maybe that's OK. It helps me remember that other people are hurting too.

In a puzzling way I am happy and sad at once. I suspect the sadness will make me prize the happiness more dearly. That's a gift from Neeley no one can ever take away.